Readymades Read and Made:

Marcel Duchamp's linguistic strategies and jokes

Part 1   1912-1916

Lyn Merrington

Dedication

To my Noel, Cameron, Isabelle and Gill for their endless patience and support.

Table of Contents

Acknowledgements

I would like to thank the University of Western Australia for its support and the University of Lille 3 for giving me exposure to living French language from 2003 to 2009. Muriel Malvoisin, now deceased, was truly the best of *voisins* and was instrumental in supporting me. Thanks to Michel Maillard, Bernadette Tillard, and Jean-Claude Dupas. I would like to thank Adeline Descamps and her family for her good humor and welcome. Sandrine Bouillon and Stefan Thouroude introduced me to *la folie linguistique des normands*, essential background for this study. Thanks to Baudoin Lebon for being *le bon pour moi* and for introducing me to Jacques Caumont, who in turn generously introduced me to Duchamp's daughter Yo Sermayer and to many Duchamp sites.

Thanks to Ian McLean for supporting my work generally.

Introduction

This study concentrates on Duchamp's development after what he describes as a key incident in his life in March 1912. This event was the request to remove his *Nude descending a staircase #2* from the 'Independents' exhibition by Albert Gleizes, and Jean Metzinger. His own brothers Jacques Villon and Raymond Duchamp Villon delivered the request. Marcel had believed them to be 'in the most advanced group of the period' and 'free.' The Nude however 'wasn't in the line that they had predicted. He said this event 'gave me a turn' and led me 'to rid myself of this milieu' and give up painting.[1]

His actions were a reaction against the French definition of an artist, which is *artiste-peintre*. De Duve has discussed the readymade *Peigne* whose title is a play on the subjunctive verb to paint, giving 'should I paint'[2].

The term artist was generally in wider use in French than

---

[1] Pierre Cabanne, *Dialogues with Marcel Duchamp*, (New York Da Capo Press, 2009) reprint of Belfond Press 1979 Edition of same name,) translation Ron Padgett, 17.

[2] Thierry De Duve, *Pictorial Nominalism : On Marcel Duchamp's Passage from Painting to the Readymade*, (Minneapolis, Oxford, University of Minnesota Press, 1991.

in English at the time so the specification of painter was added.[3] Why be a painter? Why indeed?

Many of Duchamp's works are reactions against definition and judgement particularly in relation to the visual arts. He said 'to speak of truth and real absolute judgement, I don't believe in it at all'[4].

The visual arts in French are *les Beaux arts*, literally 'the Beautiful Arts'. Duchamp stated of the readymades: 'the intention of the readymade was to get rid of this idea of the beautiful and the ugly.'[5] Once again Duchamp was reacting against a literal definition of art. Beautiful arts? No not at all! His keyword was indifference. He argued against aesthetic sensations in favor of a kind of anesthesia.[6]

1912 was important for many additional reasons. Duchamp saw Raymond Roussel's play *Impressions D'Afrique* with Guillaume Apollinaire, Francis Picabia and

---

[3] Marguerite-Marie Dubois, *Dictionnaire modern Français-Anglais*, (Paris, Larousse, 1960), 46

[4] Cabanne, 70

[5] Duchamp in interview with Philippe Colin 21 June 1967, *Marcel Duchamp Parle des Readymades*, (Paris: Echoppe, 2008), 11. My translation.

[6] Ibid., 12, 13 he argued particularly against the lack of anecdote or history that he saw in what was called retinal art at the time.

his wife Gabrielle Buffet Picabia, with whom he was secretly in love, before it closed on 10 June 1912. On 19 June, he went to Munich, via Basel, to get away from the artistic milieu he knew[7].

These important events were instrumental in his revolt and in his designation of the *readymades*.

Duchamp's background as a Norman is of utmost importance to any understanding of his work and his method. His Norman love of language games and ambiguity is paramount to any study of his 'work'. His 'work' may be a rejection of the idea of 'work' itself. The French refer to *un oeuvre d'art*, a work of art in the same way we do in English[8].

Certain characteristics of the French language make it more ambiguous and open to punning than English. Final letters of individual words are often not pronounced in French, meaning many words sound the same although their spelling and meanings are different. His own name

---

[7] These facts are in Jennifer Gough Cooper, Jacques Caumont, *Marcel Duchamp work and life: Ephemerides on and about Marcel Duchamp and Rrose Selavy*, (Massachusetts, MIT Press, 1993) Unpaginated work, events noted by date, which are not in chronological order, but by day of the year, all years together.
[8] Marguerite-Marie Dubois, *Dictionnaire modern français-anglais*, (Paris, Larousse, 1960, 496.

Duchamp's name is open to this type of interpretation, giving *du chant* 'from the song', which is apt when referencing his work, as many of his titles are puns or jokes in which the sound is paramount, and which we can hear like a song. The edition of his notes and various texts entitled *Duchamp du signe*, contains punning references to some of the most significant aspects of his work.[9] Literally translated as *Duchamp of the sign* it also reads homohonically as *du chant du cygne*, from the song of the swan, or from the swan song.[10]

There are fewer words in French than in English, meaning we place more importance on interpretation than in English. French places less stress on individual syllables, and words are more often joined together, and thus meaning slips and slides with very slight changes of tone and spacing.

I contend that the *readymades* have been largely misunderstood, due to Duchamp's use of linguistic irony and also the fact that they have been taken so seriously.

---

[9] Marcel Duchamp, *Duchamp du signe, Ecrits*, (Paris: Champs Flammarion, 1958, 1994 Edition), Preface by Michel Sanouillet, new edition augmented and reviewed with collaboration of Elmer Peterson.
[10] *Duchamp du Signe: Ecrits, Réunis et présentés par Michel Sanouillet*, (Paris, Champs Flammarion, 1974, 1994)

Duchamp stated the importance of their titles and his desire to add a verbal element to his works. He repeatedly mentioned his love of humour and his intention to introduce it into his art[11].

The word *readymade* contains the clues we need. They are read *y* made. Read and made. Duchamp coined this term in the United States in 1915[12]. As a Frenchman learning English, he would have been conscious of the Hispanic presence and of the precedence of English over other languages, particularly Spanish. '*Y*' means 'and' in Spanish[13]. Duchamp's nod to the Hispanic influence in the US has generally not been mentioned, as Anglo-centric commentary prevails. Duchamp noted this Anglo centrism and used it to his advantage, often making cheeky comments through his titles by exploiting their punning ambiguity, which would have been lost on Anglophones.

This study is as far as possible a simple explanation of Duchamp's French, his linguistic methods and jokes.

I have referred as far as possible to Duchamp's own words and to contemporary dictionaries and texts. I have

---

[11] Cabanne, 29. Katherine Kuh, *The Artist's voice, Talks with Seventeen Modern Artists*, (New York, Da Capo Press, 2000 republication of Harper and Row's 1962 Edition) 90.
[12] Cabanne, 47.
[13] Collins Gem Spanish dictionary, (Glasgow, Harper Collins, 2006), 302.

tried to avoid jargon or theoretical explanation, relying on the French language and established facts in Duchamp's history.

Marcel's Early History and Norman heritage

Marcel Duchamp was born in *Blainville-Crevon*, Normandy, a small village which remains unchanged to this day. Marcel was the fourth child in his family, born shortly after the death of his sister Jeanne, on 28th July 1887. Of the seven children born in the family three became artists. Marcel's maternal grandfather Emile Nicolle was, at Marcel's birth, considered to be one of Rouen's leading artists, a successful etcher who had been admitted to the *Beaux Arts* section of the *Exposition Internationale* in Paris[14]. His mother was described as distant and indifferent, preferring the two last born girls. She was also significantly, slightly deaf. This must have led to many *malentendus*, misunderstandings, or literally mis-hearings. The sound of a word being not quite caught, misheard, and misunderstood contributed to Marcel's appreciation for the slippery nature of the spoken word.

---

[14] Emile Nicolle, Duchamp's maternal grandfather, see Alice Goldfarb Marquis, *Marcel Duchamp: The Bachelor Stripped Bare*, (Boston, Massachusetts, MFA Publications, 2002),18.

We cannot overlook the importance of Duchamp's early environment. His father's role as a notary, part of the apparatus of the legal system, meant he was an important man in rural life, and was aware of, and active in the affairs of the region.[15] Duchamp's house is located centrally right next to that other authority, the Church. Marcel's father was well informed, and his library contained the most representative works of the preceding literary generation giving Marcel a privileged position amongst the artist friends he was later to meet in Montparnasse and Montmartre. Here, in the *champs normands,* the Norman fields of *Blainville-Crevon,* Duchamp lived the life of the *petit aristocrat.* The house is still surrounded by fields (*champs*) which fall away to a small stream.

---

[15]Eugene Duchamp was a well-respected local figure who was quite successful and on several local boards see Larry Witham, *Pablo Picasso, Marcel Duchamp and the Battle for the soul of Modern Art,* (Hanover and London, New England Press, 2013) 25,26,29. family details see Goldfarb Marquis, 19-22. The notary's role is somewhere between a Justice of the Peace and a solicitor.

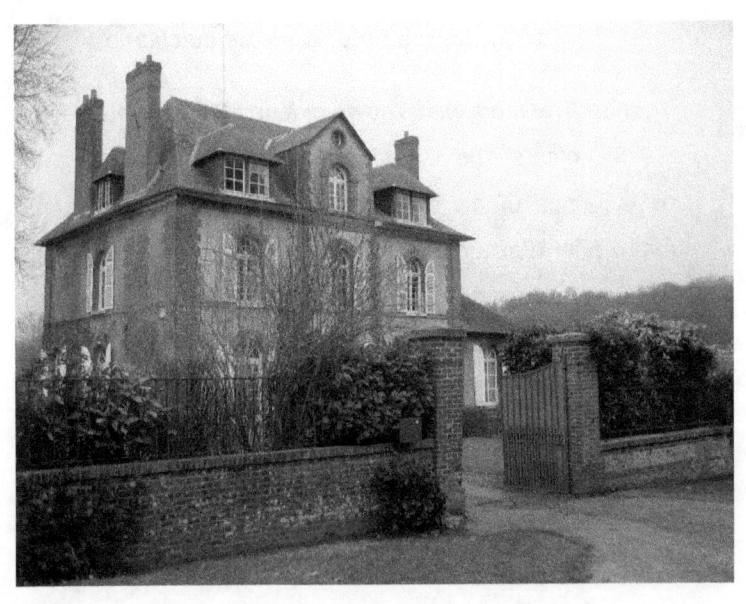

Marcel Duchamp's house Blainville-Crevon, Normandy

In the three decades since Duchamp's death, art critics and cultural commentators have made much of the name Duchamp and the ideas and connections it evokes. Bourdieu has used "Duchamp" and his name as an example for his theorization of the forces at work in the cultural "field" or *champ*. [16] Gervais and others have semantically linked the name Duchamp with that of his subsequently created female alter ego Rrose Selavy,

[16] Pierre Bourdieu, *The Field of Cultural Production: Essays on Art and Literature*, Ed and Intro by Randal Johnson, (Cambridge, Polity Press, 1993), 61.

posing (R)rose from the field, or *Rrose du champ*.[17]

Perhaps the most well-known of Marcel's word plays is his 1920 choice of the name *Rrose Selavy* for his alter ego. It is evidence of his sensitivity to semantic linkages and word play. Rather than analyzing his word play though a theoretical framework as have previous authors, this study will concentrate on the semantic and linguistic elements which may have led to Duchamp's adoption of such linguistic strategies. We will relate it to common or vernacular language, but will not attempt to make a particular 'sense' of Duchamp's œuvre or push it in a certain *sens* or direction but we will *prendre Duchamp*, take Duchamp and '*prendre du champ*', 'take a step back', and reexamine the cultural context from which he emerged[18].

As the above examples show, the name Duchamp is open to many linguistic resonances that, later in life, Duchamp made good use of. This is shown by his later use of Mar/Cel in the construction of his *Grand Verre Large Glass* or or *la Mariée mise à nu par ses célibataires même*. This work is divided into two domains – that of the MARiée

[17] Andre Gervais, *La Raie Alitée d'effets: à propos of Marcel Duchamp*, (Hurtubise, Quebec, la Salle, HMH, 1984)
[18] *Oxford Hachette French English Dictionary for windows*, 1994-1996, entry for *champ*.

and the CELibataires.[19] For the moment let us imagine Marcel growing up in the *champs normands,* the Norman fields and gradually becoming aware of the ambiguous nature of signification. His own family name *Duchamp* appears by homophony (one of his preferred methods of word play) in several common expressions which may even describe his project. As we have seen, the expression *prendre du champ* means 'to take a step back' and can also mean, by homophony, *prendre Duchamp,* 'take Duchamp' The expression *prendre du champ* is defined as « *prendre du recul, se mettre à distance pour mieux juger* » to take a step back, put oneself at a distance to better judge, which, given Duchamp's oft repeated declaration that he was not interested in the opinion of his contemporary public, but in that of the future public, is significant. *Prendre du champ* may also be used in the context of "*reculer dans le champ clos pour mieux affronter l'adversaire*" to recoil in a closed field to better affront the adversary.[20]

The importance of homophonic resonance, and of

---

[19] This conjuncture is well documented in many texts including Calvin Tomkins *Duchamp a biography,* (New York, Henry Holt and Company, 1996), 13; Jean Michel Rabaté "Duchamp's Ego", *Textual Practice,* 2010, 18:2, 229.

[20] Alain Rey, Sophie Chantreau, *Dictionnaire d'expressions et locutions,* (Paris : Le Robert, 2003),158.

idiomatic expressions will become ever more apparent during our study of Duchamp's œuvre. We will *se donner du champ*, give ourselves some elbowroom, or room to move, in our discussion of Duchamp.[21] The expression *avoir du champ*- to have some elbow room or room to move, figuratively speaking, describes his project of loosening categorical boundaries. Similarly, the expression *laisser du champ à quelqu'un* – to give someone room to maneuver resonates in relation to Duchamp's desire to liberate the artist from restrictive artistic categorizations. 'Leave Duchamp to someone' can also be heard homophonically in this expression. Thirdly, the expression *sortir du champ* – to go out of / take out of frame or out of shot in a picture, may describe his project in relation to the prevailing art and taste of his time[22]. Marcel Duchamp certainly took art out of the conventional frame within which it had been ensconced for many and opened up many new fields, or *champs*, for exploration.

What's in a name? You ask. For Duchamp there was plenty. This expression "What's in a name?" is itself rendered in French as *Le nom ne fait rien à la chose* -

---

[21] J.O. Kettridge, *French for English Idioms and Figurative Phrases*, (London, Routledge and Kegan Paul, 1940, 1976 reprint), 67.

[22] Oxford Hachette, op.cit., entry for *champ*

literally 'The name does nothing to the thing.' Through the course of this study we will see that the names Marcel chose did far from 'nothing' to the things they designated. This is particularly relevant in relation to the readymade, in French rendered *toutfait*. Duchamp's phrase "pictorial nominalism"[23] pictorial naming, is important. The names are, in many cases, the genesis of his works.

In returning to the Duchamp family name we find Marcel's older artist brothers changed their names to Jacques Villon (from Gaston Duchamp), and Raymond Duchamp-Villon (from Raymond Duchamp) after the poet François Villon. In changing their name they also sought a more urbane *nom/non de famille* "family name" or by homophony "no from the family"- essentially a denial of family.[24] In the choice of the name Villon they sought an association with *ville* or the city rather than the *champs* of the countryside. They apparently made their name change to save their father the embarrassment of association with artists. However, when it came time for Marcel to *sortir du champ normand* –to leave the Norman

---

[23] Marcel Duchamp, Note from the White box of 1914, *Salt seller*, 83, dated 1914 on the back of note. In Sanouillet, *Duchamp du signe*, 111 *une sorte de nominalisme pictural au dos*, 1914

[24] Lacan has made much of the homophony of *nom / non du père* -name / no of/from the father.

field[s] and go to Paris the question of embarrassment by association with artists was no longer an issue and he took with him his own name, and his sense of humour. Duchamp admitted his name had a poetic quality, contrasting this with his brother Gaston's' haste to change his name to Jacques Villon. 'There are periods when words lose their salt...I was sort of obligated to. [keep my name] One of us had to.'[25]

One must also wonder if the name of the town Blainville-Crevon, was a source of amusement. The second part of the name is a near homophone, a paraphone, with the geographic pun *aller à Crevant*, go to Crevant, meaning to die.[26]The name Crevon, is a homophone of the second person form of the verb to die, *crever*, so *crevons*, means we die, or in the imperative, may mean lets die. The verb *crever* may mean *crever* to burst, puncture, or colloquially to snuff it, to wear someone out, or work them to death, or *crever de rire*, to die laughing or in the expression *marche ou crève*, literally walk or die, or in English we would say sink or swim[27]. Curiously the word

---

[25] Cabanne, 90.

[26] Pierre Guiraud, *Les Locutions Francaises*, (Paris, Presses Universitaires de France, 1973), 96. aller à Crevant – mourir.

[27] Oxford-Hachette French English Dictionary for Windows, entry for *crever*.

blain in English means in French an *abcès* and the expression *crever l'abcès* literally to puncture the abscess or blain means to resolve a crisis[28].

Duchamp's interest in word play was not idiosyncratic but a common practice in Normandy and a well-established avant-gardist mode. Near Blainville is the village of Ry (incidentally homophonic with several parts of the verb to laugh *-je ris , tu ris , il rit* - I , you, he laughs and the past participle of laugh – *on a ri-* we laughed).[29] This is the town on which Gustave Flaubert based his novel *Madame Bovary*, based on the story of a local woman, who, bored with her mediocre husband and life, opted for the melodrama of a series of affairs and the accompanying debts entailed by the fineries required by such relations and romance. In this ironic masterpiece, Madame Bovary's husband responds dully to puns, spoonerisms and other games. These are Duchamp's preferred linguistic devices. Madame buys her fineries from M. Lheureux (homophonic in French with Mr Happy,

---

[28] Oxford Hachette, op.cit., entry for *abcès*. For French translation of blain, see reverso online dictionary dictionary.reverso.net/English-french/blain, accessed 1/06/2019.

[29] It would be unusual to use the past simple form of rire, ri, as laughing usually is expressed in the imperfect tense. On riait. However, one would commonly say *on rit*, we laugh, in the present familiar tone.

M. L'heureux), to whom she falls in serious debt. She eventually kills herself with arsenic rather than face her debts to Mr Lheureux, her dull life and losing her beautiful things and beautiful illusions. It is not improbable that Duchamp's father as notary had in his possession the papers concerning Delphine Delamare, on which the story of Emma (Madame Bovary) was based and whose grave is located in Ry. Monsieur Delamare was a pupil of Gustave Flaubert's father. Much has been made of Flaubert's use of the name Bovary. It has been speculated that Bovary is intended to emphasise the bovine aspect of her character. Ry the name of the town on which the story is based is included in her name – one may read, with the use of a paronym, or a slight change in sound, almost homophonically '[le] *beau va à Ry*' the beautiful one, meaning one's lover, or '*beau*' in a more general sense of the beautiful, goes to Ry. In addition one may also read Bovary as the '*[le] beau varie*' – the beautiful varies.[30] It may be going too far to say that Duchamp's exploration of aesthetic delimitations and of the impact of the "beautiful" in *Les Beaux arts*, the fine

---

[30] Jacques Caumont proposed '*le beau varie*' as a reading of this title. I am indebted to him for showing me many Duchamp sites in this area of France, and for introducing me to Duchamp's only child Yo Sermayer in her studio in Montmartre before she died.

arts stems from the title and fiction of Madame Bovary. Nevertheless, one should be aware of the real and tangible presence of Flaubert in Duchamp's milieu during his formative years. Duchamp admits the atmosphere in which he grew up was 'very Flaubertian indeed' although he did not realise this until he read Madame Bovary at sixteen.[31] Exposure to the real source of such an influential story as that of Madame Bovary with such a place name must have amused Duchamp. Certainly, *Marcel aurait ri*, Marcel would have laughed at this coincidence at Ry.

---

[31] Cabanne, 19.

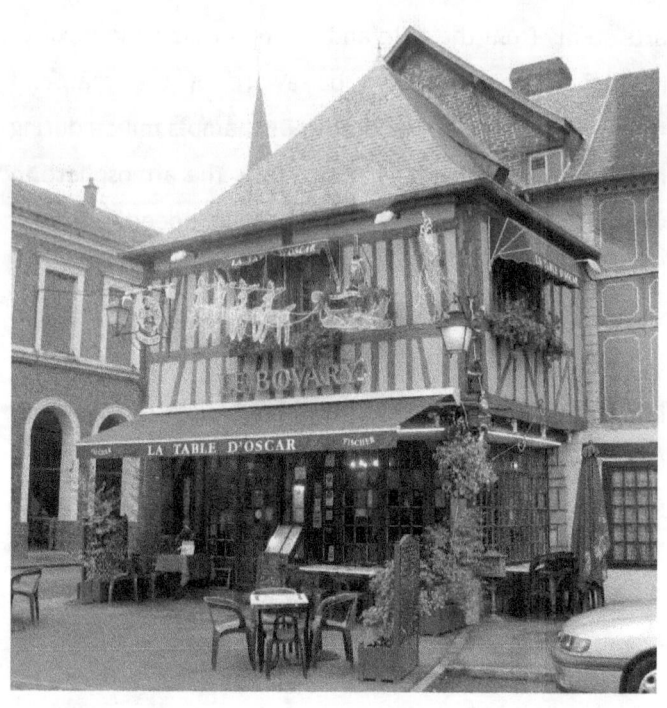

Le Bovary Hotel in Ry, Normandy. There is also a monument to Flaubert and a Bar called *Le Flaubert*, a gift shop called *Emma*, and a Pharmacy which still resembles that in Madame Bovary.

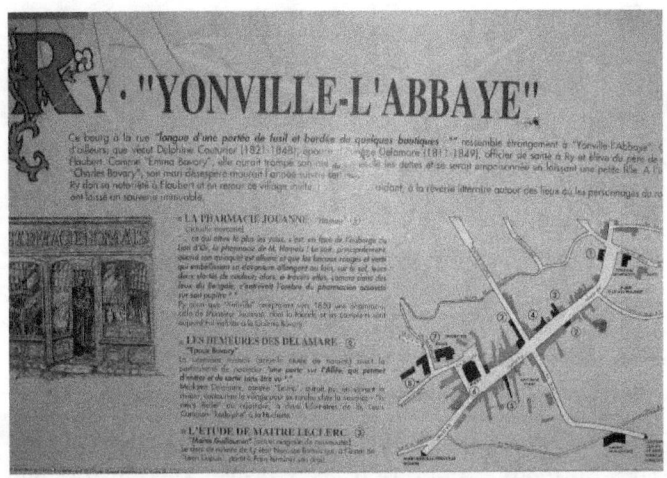

This map shows the sites in Ry which are of relevance to Flaubert's *Madame Bovary*. There is also a circuit of the surrounding towns which shows sites which are referenced in *Madame Bovary*, including Duchamp's home-town Blainville-Crevon.

Marcel must have had the impression of living in a novel. Madame Bovary was published in 1856 and Flaubert was at the height of his fame during Duchamp's youth.

The language reflects the character of Normans. They have a reputation, deserved or otherwise, of being evasive, such that the expression *"répondre en normand"* literally to reply in Norman or reply as a Norman, means

19

variously *évasivement ou de maniere ambiguë*" evasively or ambiguously[32]. One of Duchamp's preferred dictionaries, The *Littré*, defines this expression as "*ne répondre ni oui ni non*"- to answer neither yes nor no.[33] We will see throughout this study of Duchamp the importance of this aspect of his historical heritage and his tendency to avoid opposites and definitives. Duchamp was very much a Norman who used well established and popular linguistic games for different purposes.

The Normans' reputation as evasive was historically established to such an extent that from the seventeenth century *normand*, Norman, was a synonym of *madré* or *rusé*, crafty or cunning[34]. We often describe a canny fellow as *un fin normand*, literally a fine norman[35]. A *normand* is figuratively also one who cannot be trusted[36]. Similarly, a *réconciliation normande*, Norman reconciliation is a simulated reconciliation. The proverb '*un Normand a son dit et son dédit*" "a Norman has his

---

[32] *Dictionnaire d'expressions et locutions* (Paris : le Robert, 2003), 637, cited from *La Fontaine*, 1678.
[33] *Dictionnaire de la langue Francaise de E Littré*, (Paris Hachette, 1900, 761. This dictionary also has the definitions included in the above Robert.
[34] *Le Nouveau Littré*, 2003, 637.
[35] J. O. Kettridge, *French for English idioms and figurative phrases*, (London, Henley: Routeledge and Kegan Paul, first pub 1940 reissued 1996), 30
[36] *Littré*, 1900, 761.

word and his retraction" may have a historical origin in an ancient Norman law in which there was the right of retraction for twenty-four hours[37]. Certainly, we cannot overlook Duchamp's linguistic and Norman heritage in any analysis of his work[38].

Such linguistic and nonsensical games are still prevalent in Normandy. Duchamp described conversation with literary figures of the time 'a fireworks' of linguistic alliteration, puns, lies, jokes and other word games veering in different directions into sense and nonsense, between a sort of anguish and insane laughter[39].

Word games play a role in popular culture and are common in advertising campaigns and in everyday life and are present in many forms. As exemplified by the signs in the town of Ry, and in many other towns, puns abound in Duchamp's native Normandy. Normans consider themselves to have a more pronounced linguistic sense of play than your average Frenchman.

---

[37] *Dictionnaire d'expressions et locutions* le Robert, 2003, 637.
[38] These expressions also in H Hamilton, E Legros, *Dictionnaire Internationale français anglais*, (Paris, Ch Fouraut et Fils, Paris, Samson Low et Co. London, 1880) 633. They are very much of Duchamp's time.
[39] Cabanne, 24.

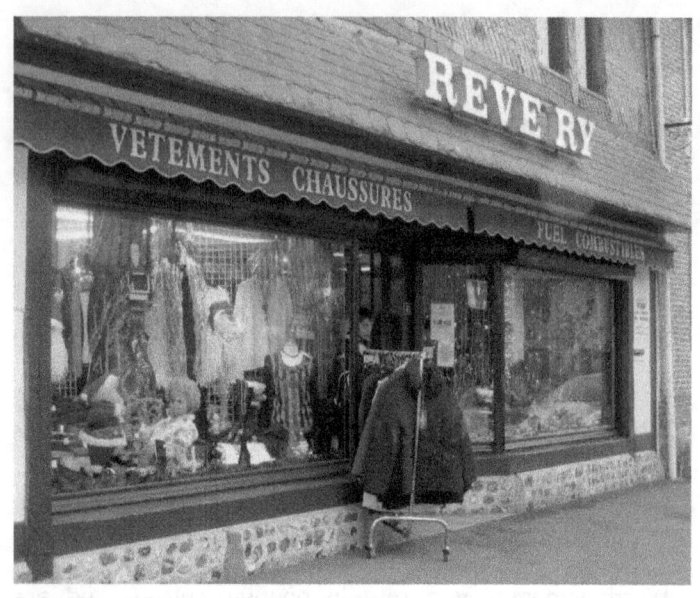

Shop in Ry, Normandy. The title is a pun on the French word *Reverie*, Daydream, or Dream Ry.

Puns and word games were also very present during Duchamp's formative years, as he mentions, in popular literature such as the *Almanac Vermot*. Such magazines carried cartoons and articles of popular interest. One such article entitled *Bizarreries de la langue française*, "Bizarre characteristics of the French language", gives instances of linguistic inconsistencies and amusing figures of speech. It notes, amongst other *bizarreries*, that French expressions allow one to 'laugh yellow' [force oneself to laugh at something one doesn't really find funny], 'see red', have 'black moods' and 'like roses/pinks' '*On peut à la fois rire jaune, voir rouge, broyer du noir et aimer les roses*'.[40] It is important to note that word games form part of the everyday culture of French people similarly to that in which they do so in English, and Duchamp's work should be considered in relation to this popular tradition.

Duchamp's reputation largely derives from his perceived injection of an intellectual content into the visual arts. This insistence on the intellectual has been responsible for a tendency to hyper-intellectualize Duchamp. Studies have concentrated on what the (often Anglophone) reader conceived the word 'intellectual' to mean. Many French people would regard an intellectual as someone who is engaged in political issues in a way in which Duchamp never was in any perceivable way. He found such commitments rather tiresome and tried to avoid them.[41] In Duchamp's statement, 'intellectual' is merely

---

[40] Sanouillet, "Marcel Duchamp and the French intellectual tradition", *Marcel Duchamp*, Eds. Anne D'Harnoncourt, Kynaston McShine, (New York: Museum of Modern Art, 1973, 1989), 51 Extract from Almanac Vermot, Thursday April 10 1919.
[41] Cabanne, 102, he says 'That's the danger in Paris. They want you to sign petitions, to get involved, *engagé* as they say. You feel obliged to follow. Cabanne: You're like Cézanne; you're afraid of being hooked. Duchamp: Yes that's it. It's the same

23

opposed to the purely visual, and to the manual. It is neither necessarily high-minded nor a referent to philosophy. The use of the word intellectual, in tandem with Duchamp's reticence to explain his art, or rather his tendency to *repondre en normand*, answer evasively, has shrouded his work in a certain intrigue and led to a situation in which a search for hermetic clues to the profound meaning of Duchamp's art has both enhanced his reputation and exponentially increased the number of highly theoretical studies on his work.[42] I do not wish to diminish the intellectual importance of Duchamp, but would like to show his (intelligent) use of elements which are other than highly 'intellectual.'

The term *intellectuel* was a relatively new term in Duchamp's youth. It was first noted in reference to Flaubert's writing. Paul Bourget, who considered Flaubert an intellectual saw the intellectual as 'playing

---

idea ...If it isn't a literary movement it's a woman; it's the same thing.

[42] Much Duchamp scholarship has been concerned with deciphering the hermetic meaning of Duchamp's work with reference to Alchemy and the fourth dimension. Duchamp stated that if he had practiced alchemy it was without being aware of it. Nevertheless, scholars continue to reveal hermetic clues as evidence of Duchamp's alchemical practices.

with thought like a child plays with poison.'[43] The term became more prominent during the Dreyfus affair of 1898 which divided France for several years and was inherently political. A group of Intellectuals submitted a manifest and were accused of acting beyond their area of expertise by others, who were themselves accused of being intellectuals, the elite 'who ask of the moral or material universe occasions of elegant and aesthetic enjoyment.'[44]

It is important to note that Duchamp considered himself a Cartesian, who had rejected Cartesianism, a defrocked Cartesian, or one who liked applying Cartesian logic and thought to painting whilst simultaneously wishing to escape them. He said: 'French education is based in strict logic. You carry this in yourself. I had to reject Cartesianism in a certain way. I don't say that you can't be both.'[45] His intellectual demeanour or his 'subordination of passion to logic, *and down to earth*

---

[43] William M Johnston, "The origin of the term Intellectuals in French Novels and Essays of the 1890s, Journal of European Studies, 1974, 44, cited from Paul Bourget, Psychologie contemporaine, Notes et portraits Gustave Flaubert *La nouvelle Revue*, 16, 15 juin 1882, p.886.

[44] Johnston, 44. From Henri Berenger « La jeunesse intellectuel et le roman français contemporain », *L'universite de Paris,* no.31 feb 1890, 28.

[45] Doré Ashton, Rencontre avec Marcel Duchamp, (Paris, L'Echoppe) 1996, 8. My translation.

good sense' was one trait Sanouillet attributed to his class background. Significantly Sanouillet also lists 'discretion, prudence, honesty, rigor of judgement, concern for efficiency, ... controlled and sly humour, and, above all, methodical doubt.' [46] However contradictory these traits may be, we should keep them in mind in the discussion of Duchamp's formative milieu and literary influences.

Duchamp admitted few influences in the visual arts stating that he preferred to be influenced by writers rather than artists[47]. He specifically mentions Rabelais, Jean-Pierre Brisset, Roussel, Alfred Jarry, Jules Laforgue, Lautréamont, Stephane Mallarmé, (and the philosophers Stirner and Phyrrho the Ancient Greek). One must also note Francois Villon, the writer after whom his brothers named themselves and who was a very popular larrikin at the time.

Duchamp said he didn't read much and never read writers fashionable at the time such as Molière or Proust[48]. He preferred the aforementioned marginal figures who disdained the conventional status of artist and poet and attacked the structure of society.[49] Given the highly

---

[46] my italics, Sanouillet, 1973, 48.
[47] Sanouillet, 1973, 126.
[48] Cabanne, 1987, 105.
[49]Sanouillet does not include Rabelais in the Duchampian

26

developed word-play evidenced in Duchamp's titles and his enigmatic use of notes it is not surprising Duchamp preferred writers who played with the figures of speech and stretched linguistic expression beyond the straightforward requirements of signification. Sanouillet describes the literary milieu of Duchamp's time: 'No longer interested in the connotative function of language, in the emotive effects to be achieved by manipulating verse... writers now began concentrating on verbal cells in their pure, denotative function, then on the anarchic development of these cells in the presence of certain catalytic agents, and finally on the rupture of the conjunctive tissue that had untied them ever since language had come into being.'[50]

This study will show how Duchamp used language itself, particularly popular verbal elements in the genesis of his visual works. In doing so we will try to keep in mind his friend Henri Pierre Roché's remark *"Je me mefie des normands comme Duchamp, je sais que Duchamp peut m'avoir."*[51] I distrust Normans like Duchamp, I know that he can have/con me.

---

constellation, but also adds Joris-Carl Huysmans, whose novel *A Rebours,* or in reverse, was in fashion at the time.
[50] Sanouillet, 1973, 51-52.
[51] Henri Pierre Roché cited in Sanouillet, « Preface de 1958 Edition » *Duchamp du Signe*, 1994 Edition, 18.

Broyeuse de Chocolat: The Chocolate Grinder, 1913.

The *Broyeuse de Chocolat* is one of the only works of which Duchamp created several versions. It is included here as a key work as it marks Duchamp's transition from *artiste-peintre* to one who used other techniques. Duchamp claims he was inspired by a *Broyeuse de Chocolat* in a street in Rouen: 'We used to go to Rouen with the family for the holidays, I saw the chocolate grinder in Rouen in a *chocolatier* in Rue des Carmes.'[52] Duchamp made two versions of the *Broyeuse de chocolat*, The first *Chocolate Grinder* is completely painted, whereas in the second edition a sewing thread is not only stuck with paint and varnish but is sewn into the canvas at all the intersections.

Duchamp continues, saying in October 1913 he moved to rue Saint-Hippolyte in Paris. There he drew on the walls the placement of the *Broyeuse* and the first sketches for the work he called his *Grand Verre*, Large Glass, or '*La mariée mise à nu par ses célibataires, même*'. The Bride stripped bare by her Bachelors, even.[53] The construction

---

[52] Cabanne, 37.
[53] Cabanne, 37.

of the second *Broyeuse*, with the thread is his first attempt at using thread with paint. Duchamp intended this technique to be 'like an architectural dry rendering.'[54] He later used this technique in construction of the *Grand Verre, the* Large Glass or *La mariée mise à nu*...where he used lead thread to outline the forms. This and its timing are important considerations in the development of his oeuvre.

The *Broyeuse de chocolat* is an integral part of the lower domain of the *Grand Verre*, or *Mariée*..., which he called the bachelor domain. Here in the bachelor domain the bachelor machine holds moulds of different types, *les moules maliques*, the malish moulds. This is a neologic adverbial joke on the words *male*, male and *malish which evokes the French word, malicieux, meaning, malicious or mischievous*[55]. The mould forms are like those one would use in moulding chocolate shapes. They represent different males or roles they played in society, such as a soldier, Gendarme, Flunky, department store delivery boy, Busboy, Priest, Undertaker, policeman, Stationmaster[56]. The suggestion is that society moulds

---

[54] Arturo Schwarz, *Complete works of Marcel Duchamp*, (London, Thames and Hudson, 1997) Vol. 1, 133, 134.

[55] Oxford Hachette, entries for *malice, malicieux,*

[56] Arturo Schwarz, *Complete works of Marcel Duchamp*, (Paris: Thames and Hudson, 1997) volume 2, 632

males into the particular forms it needs. Duchamp said they were meant to be coffin like.

The *moules maliques* are suspended and turning over a base which is another *Broyeuse de chocolat*. However, instead of being chocolate moulds, Duchamp's notes show he intended the *moules maliques* to be moulds for parcels of gas, he writes '*Gaz: Coupé en morceaux*' 'Gas cut into pieces.' [57] In English we speak of cutting the gas or in French *couper le gaz*. Hence the idea of cutting is one of Duchamp's absurd jokes playing on this common expression of the time.

Gas was a newly available commodity at the time, as evidenced by the later *EAU ET GAZ A TOUS LES ETAGES*, *WATER AND GAS AT ALL LEVELS*. This is a reference to a sign often erected on buildings to advertise the new conveniences in Paris in the 1890s. Duchamp reproduced this as the cover of the deluxe versions of Robert Lebel's 1959 book *Sur Marcel Duchamp*. The panel relates to the expression '*il y a de l'eau dans le gaz*', meaning 'people aren't getting on' or 'there are problems'. This expression is very much of Duchamp's time, as cars and machinery were becoming a part of everyday life. It gives an image of a machine spluttering along inefficiently due

---

[57] Duchamp, *Notes*, (Paris: Flammarion, 1999), 62.

to contaminated gas. The production of Lebel's book encountered constant difficulties and was delayed when the first publisher lost the manuscript, Lebel added extra details at the last minute, and was forced to change publishers and translators. Hence, the publication spluttered along at all stages[58].

Keeping in mind the image of male moulds turning on an apparatus suspended over a chocolate grinder, one must recall the most common expressions related to *chocolat*. Some commentators have noted the expression '*etre chocolat*' meaning '[t]o feel frustrated or let down, particularly in relation to the bachelor forms and sexual frustration.'[59] Strutz gives the example '*j'ai été chocolat quand il est parti au concert avec une autre. I felt let down when he went to the concert with someone else.*'[60] Duchamp's notes certainly reflect this idea for the *Broyeuse "Le célibataire broie son chocolat lui-même'*, the bachelor grinds his own chocolate. He noted that he wished this phrase to be in the form of an advertisement in the text he intended to create to accompany the *Grand*

---

[58] For details of the publication of Sur Marcel Duchamp see Paul B. Franklin, "Headline Duchamp" *Etant Donné*, no.7. 2006, 140-171.

[59] Schwarz, vol. 1, 153.

[60] Henri Strutz, *Dictionary of French Slang and Colloquial expressions*, (New York, Barron, 2009), 83.

verre.[61]

In relation to the *Broyeuse de Chocolat*, the central element in the bachelors' domain of the Large glass, no commentators have to my knowledge noted the related expression *faire chocolat*, to make chocolate, which is literally what a chocolate grinder does. Henri Strutz' Dictionary of French slang has the following definition '*Chocolat*, Chocolate, *faire chocolat*, idiom, To deceive, *il a reussi a me faire chocolat*, He succeeded in putting one over on me.'[62] In the large Glass the *moules maliques*, the bachelor molds, turn around on the chocolate grinder and are forever kept separated from the *Mariée*, frustrated and moulded according to the roles required by society. The *Mariée* and society 'deceived' or 'put one over' on the bachelors.

Moreover, the *Broyeuse de chocolat* gave Duchamp inspiration for his method. To '*Faire chocolat*' 'make chocolate' describes Duchamp's method. He constantly and mischievously 'put one over' on spectators. He delights in using his French language to dupe the mostly Anglophone spectators in speculation about what it all

---

[61] Duchamp, *Notes*, 73. *
[62] Henri Strutz, 83.

may mean.

The Broyeuse has 3 *meules*. In Duchamp's notes the word meules is emphasised[63]. *Meules* are grindstones. However, the word meules also means haystacks[64]. Here, when seeing this note, it is impossible to dismiss the idea that Duchamp was referencing *meules*, particularly Monet's haystacks which Duchamp so despised. One must know Monet often painted in or near Rouen, his famous series of the facade of Rouen cathedral being a case in point. The *Rue des Carmes*, where Duchamp saw the inspiring chocolate grinder, runs along the façade of the famous *Cathedral Notre Dame* to the exact spot where Monet painted his series. Hence, there is a very close correlation between Monet's *meules* haystacks and Duchamp's *meules*, grindstones.

One notes that there were three brothers in the Duchamp family who were artists. The reference to the *meules*, the haystacks, and the three grindstones of the chocolate grinder turning and making *chocolat* evokes these three brothers' reaction to Monet's *meules*. Not only Marcel but also his brothers Jacques Villon and Raymond

---

[63] Duchamp Notes, 73. The underlining is clearer in *Duchamp du Signe suivi de Notes*, revue et corrigé par Anne Sanouillet, et Paul B Franklin, (Paris: Flammarion, 2008), 323, as in the 1999 Edition of notes underlined words are rendered in italics.
[64] Oxford Hachette, entry for *meule*.

Duchamp-Villon and the lesser cubists despised the 'retinal' quality of impressionism prevalent at the time. The term 'retinal' was not of Marcel's invention, but was referenced from Gleizes and Metzinger's treatise *Du Cubisme*, published in 1912[65].

Duchamp clearly often uses linguistic ambiguity and idiomatic expressions to *faire chocolat*, deceive and 'put one over on us' all throughout his career. His linguistic play shows the slippery nature of definition, judgement, and hierarchies, particularly in relation to the visual arts.

---

[65] Albert Gleizes, Jean Metzinger, *Du Cubisme*, (Paris: Eugène Figuières, 1912) The idea of the artwork being completed by the spectator was also expressed by Gleizes and Metzinger in *Du Cubisme*. See Mark Antliff and Patricia Dee Leighton, *Cubism and Culture*, (London, Thames and Hudson, 2001) See also Peter Brooke,
http://www.peterbrooke.org.uk/a&r/Du%20Cubisme/Part%20two/duchamp, accessed 19/09/2019

Roue de bicyclette: Bicycle Wheel, 1913

We know one of the first readymades as Bicycle wheel. Cursorily described it comprises the upturned front fork of a bicycle, with a wheel inserted into a hole in a white stool. Duchamp spoke of enjoying the movement of the wheel similarly to the way one watches a fire.

Caumont and Cooper propose that it is a tribute to Raymond Roussel, as it is a wheel *une roue*, on what we may call a *selle*, a stool. 'Is it entirely fortuitous that , when fixed together, the two elements "Roue" (Wheel) and "selle" stool become a portrait or homage to one of the men he admired the most at the time for his "delirium of imagination" Raymond Roussel.'[66] Duchamp saw Roussel's play *Impressions D'Afrique* with Apollinaire, Picabia, and his wife Gabrielle Buffet Picabia, in 1912 after his falling out with his brothers and the Cubists over the rejection of his Nude descending a staircase #2. Roussel self-funded this play as he believed the public would appreciate his genius if they heard his words rather

---

[66] Jacques Caumont, Jennifer Gough-Cooper, *Ephemerides*, non- paginated, entry for 1964, 4 June, Thursday Milan.

than just read them from a page. Hence the sound of Roussel's words, and the puns one hears are fundamental to an understanding of his work.

Similarly, Duchamp emphasized the importance of the verbal aspect of the readymades: 'instead of describing the object like a title, [the inscription] was meant to carry the mind of the spectator towards other regions more verbal.'[67]

Duchamp admired Roussel for his originality. He said of him: He is 'the only man in the last 30 years who started from a clean slate... no influence that I could detect. He puns a lot. Puns are considered low, low everywhere, in English as well as in French. And he was using a low pun'[68] 'From his Impressions D'Afrique [sic] I got the general approach. This play of his ... helped me greatly on one side of my expression. I saw at once that I could use Roussel as an influence. I felt that as a painter it was much better to be influenced by a writer than another painter. And Roussel showed me the way."[69]

---

[67] Schwarz, 45, cited from Duchamp "Apropos of Readymades"
[68] Duchamp in Calvin Tomkins, *Marcel Duchamp: the afternoon Interviews*, (New York: Badlands unlimited, 2013), 91.
[69] Cavin Tomkins, Duchamp, A Biography, Tomkins, 91 cited from Marcel Duchamp, *letters to Marcel Jean*, p.72., Munich Silke Schriber, 1987. In this letter he claims to have seen the

Roussel's work makes use of the arbitrary form of language; however, the way he created his work is far from arbitrary. He worked to a strict set of rules and made use of intricate word games. The most comprehensively documented of his techniques is what he called his *procédé* or procedure. He based this on a series of puns, homophonies and near homophonies (what Foucault calls the *à peu près* – the almost)[70]. Roussel's developed his procédé from his earliest writings.[71] He would take a carefully chosen sentence and change one letter in that sentence. French has more inherent ambiguity than English, so with the change of one letter in one sentence it was possible to change the meaning of all the other words in that sentence. *Impressions d'Afrique* is based on the phrases '*Les lettres du blanc sur les bandes du vieux billiard*' 'The chalk letters on the stripes of the old billiard table', which becomes with a change of one letter *b* to *p* '*Les lettres du blanc sur les*

---

play with Apollinaire but there is some doubt as to whether this is true.

[70] Michel Foucault, "7Propos sur le 7eme Ange", *La Grammaire Logique*, *La Science de Dieu*, Paris, Claude Tchou Editeur, 1970, p.xiii.

[71] *Parmi Les Noirs,* and the other *Textes de Grande Jeunesse* It is a pity he did not publish these early in his career as the technique is at least visible and would have given the reader an inkling of his intention.

bandes du vieux pillard' 'The white man's letters about the old pillager's band [of men]'.[72] Roussel then wove the meanings of the words in the sentence into a story.

He would then take words associated with those in the first sentence, for example, from *billiard* he took the word *queue*. *Queue* is a cue used in the game of billiards. But as Roussel states, in French, it also means a train of a garment, which he then incorporated into the story as Talou's cape. 'Thus amplifying the procedure, I sought new words related to the word billiard, always taking them in a sense other than that which first presents itself, and each time that gave me a new additional creation.'[73] Queue also means, as in English a queue or a line of people, a tail as in an animal's tail, the handle of a cooking pot, the stem of a flower or fruit, and is also slang for penis, but Roussel does not use this aspect[74]. I won't expand upon this here.

Roussel's writing is excruciating to read. He intentionally avoided all expression of emotion, so it comprises long disinterested descriptions of weird inventions and fantastic imaginings generated by the words and their

---

[72] Raymond Roussel, *Comment J'ai ecrit certains de mes livres*, (Paris, Gallimard, 1979), 13

[73] Roussel, 13.

[74] Oxford Hachette, entry for *queue*.

multiple meanings. Homophonies abound in *Impressions D'Afrique*. The images Duchamp saw in the play would have functioned both as homophonies and as rebuses. Whilst most of the audience was outraged by *Impressions D'Afrique* as they desperately tried to make conventional sense of it, Duchamp with his Norman sensitivity to language understood the linguistic conjuncture in the homophonies of a *grand ver*, a large worm, which was shown in a large glass, un *grand verre* and no doubt many other images. He said he was able to associate the text with the show when he read it afterwards. He insists that the way Roussel challenged language corresponded to the way he was challenging painting[75]. Simple *nominalism picturale*, picture naming gave him the clues he needed to decipher Roussel's technique. Duchamp speaks of *Nominalism pictural*, pictorial nominalism, several times in his notes. Thierry De Duve has explored this philosophically in relation to Duchamp's readymades[76]. Nominalism derives from the latin *nomen* name. John Stuart Mill summarized it as a belief that there is nothing general except names.

(Roussel was gay, had strict rules for living, and travelled

---

[75] Cabanne, 34.

[76] Thierry De Duve *Pictorial nominalism: On Duchamp's passage from painting to the readymade*, (Minneapolis, University of Minneapolis Press 1991).

widely in a caravan. I interpret his *procédé* which functions by changing one letter to give a different meaning, and with the use of homopho*n*ies as his way of negotiating the homopho*b*ies of the time.)

Rebuses are allusional devices that use pictures to represent words or parts of word. They were a favorite form of heraldic expression in the middle ages, and very much part of the writer Francois Villon's world. Rebuses have long been used as part of French children's word games when they are learning to read and recognize syllables. A simple example of a rebus in a children's publication includes a picture of a cat, un *chat*, (the t is mute) and a picture of skin, *peau*, to make the word *cha peau* – hat[77].

I contend that Duchamp's *readymades* are rebuses which are meant to be read, *y* [and] made, as *y* is Spanish for the word 'and'[78]. The readymades often use idiomatic

---

[77] A recent children's publication *J'aime Rire*, (Paris, Bayard, no.14) 2019, its title is itself a pun on another publication *J'aime Lire*, It includes several quite complex rebuses containing up to 27 objects to be deciphered into a sentence. It is intended for 7 to 11year-old children. Similar word games abounded in the *Almanach Vermot*, one of Duchamp's contemporary magazines and which he cited on several occasions.

[78] See Glyn Thompson, Julian Spalding, "Did Marcel Duchamp Steal Elsa's Urinal" *The Art Newspaper, International Edition*

expressions or *idiotismes* as their basis and play many types of word games[79]. Puns, spoonerisms, reversals, anagrams and other word games abound. However, these have not been adequately explained to an anglophone audience.

In returning to the bicycle wheel if we simply name what we see, or use pictorial nominalism, we see a *selle* may be a stool in both senses of the word in English, hence continuing the use of common expressions and the vulgar toilet humour theme Duchamp so loved. *Selle* was a commonly used word as evidenced by a listing in an 1880 dictionary '*avoir le cul sur la selle*' literally 'to have your arse on the saddle or stool', meaning to be seated[80].

Duchamp's love of the vulgar is clear in his notes in which he turned a common expression '*tout à leur gout*', 'everyone to his taste', in a paronym or *à peu pres*, into *Tout à l'égout*, all to the sewer[81]. In continuing

---

issue 262, 3 Nov 2014. This article claims the readymades are rebuses, but they do not identify the Spanish link.

[79]*Oxford Hachette Dictionary for Windows* (Oxford, Paris: Oxford Hachette co-publication, 1994-96) 'idiom: (linguistics) phrase: idiom, *idiotisme*

[80] Emile Littré, *Dictionnaire de la langue francaise*, (Paris Hachette et Cie, 1883), vol 1, 928

[81] Marcel Duchamp, *Duchamp du Signe*, Paris, Flammarion, 1994, p.163, original text TOUTALEGOUT SONT DANSLANATURE (all to the sewer are in nature) Pun on the expression all tastes

Duchamp's toilet humour, we see, '*aller à la selle*' means to 'have a bowel movement'. Duchamp is playing with the movement of the bicycle wheel here. Furthermore, the chair of the Bicycle wheel could be described simply as a *chaise percée*, a pierced chair, as it is pierced by the fork of the bicycle wheel. A *chaise percée* in US English is a commode[82].

We also understand the word *selle* as a saddle, a particular cut of meat, a commode, and significantly, a sculptors' turntable[83]. Here in placing a turning wheel on a *selle*, Duchamp is transforming the *selle* of the sculptor's turntable, on which the artwork is created, into an artwork and changing the orientation of its movement. He has '*abordé la sculpture sur un nouvel angle*, literally approached sculpture from a new angle or with the addition of the spinning wheel 'put a new spin' on the art of sculpture[84].

---

are in nature. This was a 1961 inscription on an engraving in the form of a rebus in the album of contemporary engraving *Surrealism between two world wars* Milan, Galleria Schwarz 1961

[82] Marguerite- Marie Dubois, Dictionnaire Moderne Français-Anglais, (Paris, Larousse, 1960), 117.

[83] Oxford Hachette, entry for *selle*. These meanings are also present in Littré, 1900, 1089.

[84] Oxford Hachette entry for spin.

Pharmacie: Pharmacy, 1914

This readymade is what Duchamp called a rectified readymade based on a small reproduction of a sentimental winter landscape by the Swiss artist, Sophie de Niederhausern, which he claimed to have purchased in an artists' supply shop. He said the idea for this came to him when he was travelling back to Rouen to visit his family in January 1914 from Paris. Marcel has merely painted two little lights in the background, coloring one red and one green, like flasks in a chemist's shop, called it *Pharmacie* and signed it.[85]

Duchamp often spoke of adding titles as adding color: '*au sens figuré du mot. C'est une couleur verbal*', ... in the figurative sense of the word. It is verbal color.[86] French has a similar understanding of colorful language as we do in English to describe what may be considered bad or less

---

[85] Jacques Caumont, Jennifer Gough Cooper, *Ephemerides*, MIT press, 1993, unpaginated book entry for 4 April 1914
[86] Philippe Colin, *Marcel Duchamp parle des Readymade*, (Paris, Echoppe, 2008), 19.

than polite language.[87] The adjective *coloré*, colored may also be used to describe something that has '*an apparance capable de seduire, de tromper*', an appearance, capable of seducing, or fooling[88].

Duchamp told Breton that the two colored dots were meant to be "two tiny figures, one red the other green, walking towards each other in the distance'.[89] Schwarz claims this work is a reference to his sister Suzanne and Duchamp's incestuous feelings for her. Her first husband, Charles Desmares, was a pharmacist.[90]

The red and green traverse his oeuvre in different ways both physically and linguistically in bilingual puns. The red/read of the *read y mades*, is itself a pun on the idea of reading these 'works.'[91] The French word green, *vert*,

---

[87]www.collinsdictionary.com/dictionary/english-french/colourful.

[88] Littré, 1900, 197.

[89]*https://www.toutfait.com/unmaking_the _museum/Pharmacy.html* « Pharmacie or pharmacy » cites Goldfarb Marquis, 96. This article mentions some scholarly conjecture about the actual colors of the dots, whether the green one is in fact green or yellow. However, Duchamp said it was green in a 1967 interview with Philippe Collin, 18.

[90] Schwarz, 189.

[91] There is some conjecture as to whether the readymades were simply found manufactured objects or were individually made. Rhonda Roland Sheerer believes they were all made by Duchamp. See Toutfait https://www.toutfait.com/issues/issue_3/collections/rrs/she arer.htm accessed 21/01/ 2019

is a well-known homophone of the words *vers*, towards, or *vers*, a line of a poem, *ver* a worm, and a *verre* glass or a glass. Indeed, his *Mariée mise à nu par ses célibataires, même*, which he referred to as his *Grand Verre*, Large Glass, encompasses this in its title. His titles and his puns can be read as *vers* verses or lines in a poem. Furthermore, if we look at the color green, *verte* in the feminine form this brings up the expression '*en dire de vertes*- to tell spicy or risqué stories.' These abound in Duchamp's oeuvre as sex abounds often disguised in risqué puns, or suggestive objects such as *Feuille de vigne*, vine leaf[92].

Argot or slang was often called *la langue verte*, literally green language[93]. Certainly, Duchamp made good use of slang throughout his career. One of the titles from a later work the *objet dard*, is a pun on the highbrow naming of an *objet d'art*, *an art object*, and *dard*, being slang for a penis[94].

---

[92] *Feuille de vigne* female fig leaf, 1950.

[93] Jules Lermina Henri Leveque, *Dictionnaire francais-argot à l'usage des gens du monde qui veulent parler correctement la langue Verte*, (Paris, Les Editions de Paris, 1991, reprint of Edition of same name Paris Charcornac, 1900. Dard is listed here.

[94] Leveque, 98, also *Dictionnaire du Francais Argotique et Populaire*, (Paris, Larousse, 2006), 69.

The color green abounds in his oeuvre, including in his *Boite Verte*, and in the *Signed Sign* from the Hotel Green.

Ver resonates in the expression *'etre nu comme un ver'* to be stark naked. Duchamp's most famous nude did not, however appear to be nude, rather appeared to be a construction of abstract shapes.[95]

---

[95] Oxford Hachette, entry for *ver*.

Hérisson: Bottle Rack, 1914

Duchamp called the bottle rack a *readymade aidé*, an assisted readymade, or a readymade at a distance, as he designated this a *readymade* in a letter to his sister Suzanne on 15th January 1916. He was living in New York and bottle racks were not a common item, as they were in his native Normandy. She had been clearing out his flat in Paris. He said he had 'purchased it as a readymade sculpture'. He explains further saying that in New York he has purchased objects 'in the same flavour', treats them as 'readymade', signs them and adds an inscription in English. 'I will give you some examples', he continues. 'For example I have a large snow shovel at the foot of which I have written: *In advance of the broken arm..*, don't struggle too much to understand the meaning, romantic or Impressionist or Cubist — that has nothing to do with it.

His instructions for the bottle rack continue "take for yourself this bottle rack, I make of it a readymade at a distance. Inscribe at the bottom, inside the bottom circle in small letters painted with an oil paint brush in white lead paint the inscription which, I will give you afterwards

49

and you will sign it with the same writing as follows: [*d'après*] according to Marcel Duchamp."[96]

Unfortunately, the inscription and the readymade have been lost so no inscription can be verified. Didier Semin sees the cartoon, with an accompanying text as the paradigm for Duchamp's works. From his earliest works language gives sense to, or underlines the nonsense in Duchamp's works. However even though the inscription has been lost we can still ascertain what Duchamp was doing with the language he applied to this object.

The title he chose for this object *Hérisson*, or hedgehog is a common name for an '*égouttoir à bouteilles*, a bottle drainer'.[97]

Caumont and Gough-Cooper see this as a play on words, with the common name for this common Norman object, an *égouttoir*, which is literally a drop remover. It is a pun on the words *goutte* drop and *goût*, taste. An *égoûtoir* is the epitome of non-taste, or a taste remover[98]. There is

---

[96] Original French manuscript reproduced in Didier Semin, *Duchamp : Le Paradigm du dessin d'humour*, Kunsthalle Marcel Duchamp, 2015, 16,17. Semin sees the cartoon, with text accompanying as the paradigm for Duchamp's work. In English Jennifer Gough Cooper et Jacques Caumont *Ephemerides*, 15 January 1916, unpaginated.

[97] Oxford Hachette, entry for *hérisson*.

[98] Gough Cooper, Caumont, 15 January 1916 unpaginated

only a very small difference in pronunciation between the words *goût* and *goutte*, and the addition of the suffix *oir*, means the t of *goût* is pronounced so this is entirely feasible.

Given Duchamp's oft declared desire to remove taste from artworks this is clearly what Duchamp was getting at: he said:

'Taste gives a sensuous feeling, not an aesthetic emotion. Taste presupposes a domineering onlooker who dictates what he likes and dislikes and translates it into "beautiful" and "ugly". Quite differently, the "victim" of an "aesthetic echo" is in a position comparable to a man in love or a believer who dismisses automatically his demanding ego and helplessly submits to a pleasurable and mysterious constraint. While exercising his taste he adopts a commanding attitude, when touched by the esthetic revelation, the same man, almost in an ecstatic mood, becomes receptive and humble.'[99]

However, despite this overarching and controlling role of *goût*, taste, he wishes to banish it from his art, along with

---

[99] Marcel Duchamp, *Paroles D'Artistes*, Marcel Duchamp (Paris, Fage, 2018), 4 from the Western Round Table on Art, San Francisco, 1949. Cited in B Marcadé, *La vie à credit*, (Paris, Flammarion, 2007)

any submission to an esthetic.

'The choice of these "readymades" was never dictated by esthetic delectation. This choice was based on a reaction of visual indifference with at the same time a total absence of good or bad taste.'[100]

Furthermore, Duchamp declared the choice of a readymade allowed him 'to reduce the idea of aesthetic consideration to the choice of the mind, not to the ability or cleverness of the hand.'[101]

Duchamp also plays on the correlation between *goût* taste and *l'égout,* the sewer, in his play on the expression *tout à leur goût,* meaning 'each to his own taste'[102]. In a paraphone he writes *tout à l'égout,* all to the sewer. Certainly, much of Duchamp's humour is what we call toilet humour, however this aspect of his work has been

---

[100] Ibid., 30, cited from "The Art of Assemblage", during a symposium directed by William C Seitz. New York, 1961.

[101] Schwarz, 615, cited from an interview with Harriet, Sidney and Carrol Janis in D'Harnoncourt and Mc Shine, Eds, Marcel Duchamp, 275.

[102] Marcel Duchamp, *Duchamp du Signe*, Paris, Flammarion, 1994, p.163, original text TOUTALEGOUT SONT DANSLANATURE (all to the sewer are in nature) Pun on the expression all tastes are in nature. This was a 1961 inscription on an engraving in the form of a rebus in the album of contemporary engraving *Surrealism between two world wars* Milan, Galleria Schwarz 1961.

down-played in preference for an 'intellectual' interpretation of his work.

A contemporary dictionary notes *hérisson*, or hedgehog is used in a familiar language to describe person with a difficult character[103]. Was this in some way a self-portrait, Duchamp having been seen to be difficult, in artistic circles for not following the trajectory his peers had mapped out? We shall never know.

Other contemporary expressions involving bottles include *etre dans la bouteille, etre dans le complot, dans l'intrigue*, to be in the bottle, to be in the plot, to be in on the intrigue. *N'avoir rien vu que par le trou d'une bouteille, ne pas connaitre les choses*, to have seen nothing but through the hole of a bottle, to not know about things.[104]

The phallic nature of the bottlerack has been noted by many: 'the obvious sexual (namely phallic) symbolism of this work need not be emphasized...'[105] Duchamp stated on many occasions his preference for eroticism over other 'isms' stating that sexuality and eroticism was 'the basis

---

[103] A Beaujean *Dictionnaire de la langue française*, (Paris, Littré. 1900)
[104] Ibid., 116.
[105] Schwarz, 189.

of everything and no one talks about it.'[106]

[106] Cabanne, 1987, 88.

Snow Shovel: In advance of the broken arm, 1915

One of the first ready-mades was a snow shovel which Duchamp named *In advance of the Broken arm*. This was bought in 1915 when Duchamp was sharing a studio with Jean Crotti in the Lincoln Arcade building in New York. They went to a hardware store and for the first time in their lives saw a snow shovel. Crotti carried it back to the studio over his shoulder[107]. Crotti was later to say: "As an artist I consider that shovel the most beautiful object I have ever seen"[108]. However, Duchamp clearly thought those who admired aesthetic beauty of the readymades had misunderstood. He later said of those who admired the aesthetic beauty of the objects he chose as readymades

"When I discovered the readymades I thought to discourage aesthetics ... I threw the bottle rack and the

---

[107] Witham, 119.

[108] Jean Crotti cited in Schwarz, 636 cited from Nicola Greeley-Smith, "Cubist depicts love in Brass and Glass, *The Evening World*, New York, April 4 1916, 3, reprinted in Rudolf E Kuenzli, Ed, *New York Dada*, Willis Locker and Owens, 1986, 135-7.

urinal in their faces as a challenge and now they admire them for their aesthetic beauty."[109]

When Duchamp bought this in New York it was not at all a common object in France. As with all of Duchamp's titles there has been much speculation as to its meaning. It has been linked to Mallarmé, by the lexical link of *mal* – pain and the broken arm.

If we consider the object simply, if we read the read y made, we can describe it as a show shovel. Although a shovel is usually translated as *une bêche* this object is commonly described in French as a *Pelle à neige*. A snow spade. Duchamp himself describes it as a *pelle à neige* in his 1916 letter to his sister Suzanne[110]. This disjuncture between *beche*, shovel and *pelle*, spade, immediately highlights the slippery ambiguous nature of language and above all, of translation. It also calls up the English expression "To call a spade a spade" which in French is rendered *appeler un chat un chat*, literally to call a cat a cat or *dire le mot et la chose*, to say the word and the

[109] Witham, 223, Duchamp cited in Hans Richter, *Dada art and Anti Art*, New York, McGraw Hill, 1977, 207-8.
[110] Didier Semin, *Duchamp le paradigm de l'humour*, Kunsthalle Marcel Duchamp, 2015, 16,17

thing[111]. Evidently what we call in English a shovel may in French be a spade. So it is correct to call a spade a shovel. One must note Duchamp's astute choice in this object. It articulates his project with the *readymades* and many of his other works succinctly. It highlights the folly of definition and of language.

The *Snow Shovel* plays on Duchamp's delight in word games and particularly in idiomatic expressions or, as they are so aptly called in French *idiotismes*. In English we say 'what's in a name?' The closest French equivalent expression *le nom ne fait rien à la chose*, literally 'the name does nothing to the thing' is here questioned, shown to be idiotic, and wrong. Clearly, in naming it a readymade Duchamp immediately takes the *snow shovel* out of the realm of the ordinary everyday object and inserts it into the realm of art. His authority as a French-American artist with pedigree, history and reputation means that what he decrees art, indeed becomes such. *Le nom **fait tout** à la chose*. The name does everything to the thing. *Un objet **tout -fait*** – a *readymade* object becomes art. He, and the art theorists that gave his action currency, with time, extend the realm of art

[111]Francois Denoeu, David Sices, Jacqueline Sices, 2001 French and English idioms 2nd Edition, 2001 *Idiotismes francais et anglais*, 2eme edition, 1996, Barron, Hauppauge, New York, p.425.

objects and demonstrate that simply by naming one can *tout faire*, do everything, to an object *tout-fait*, to a *readymade* object.

When Duchamp returned to his studio with the snow shovel, he suspended it on a piece of wire so that it was mobile and could have been rolled around or turned around. Given Duchamp's reputation as a bit of a ladykiller the phrase *rouler une pelle*, or do a French kiss has been mentioned in relation to this object so this is quite probably one of Duchamp's implied meanings. Other *idiotismes* also come to mind. *Ramasser une pelle*, literally 'gather a shovel' or *Prendre un pelle*, take a shovel, also means to take a fall, flop, or look stupid in doing something[112]. How Duchamp must have chuckled when Schwarz, with his crazy theories about Duchamp and his incestuous love for his sister Suzanne, started to *ramasser des pelles*, gather snow shovels in replica to sell them in limited editions[113].

---

[112] Strutz, op.cit., p.290 *J'ai ramassé un gadin dans le metro et une pelle au boulot*. I had a fall in the subway and got egg on my face at work.

[113] Schwarz's Editions were made with Duchamp's cooperation. However, Duchamp was too much of a gentleman to ever counter Schwarz's theories, much to his wife Teeny's consternation.

Tiré à Quatre Épingles: Pulled at four pins, 1915

The title of this work dated 1915 is a literal translation of the French expression '*tiré à quatre épingles*, or as we would say 'dressed up to kill' or dressed to the nines, or the Us expression of the time, dressed to the teeth.'[114]

At this time Duchamp was discovering a new language and interested in not only in literal translations but also those hard to master idiomatic expressions.

Schwarz sees an autobiographical quality in this object, as Duchamp 'always managed to be quite elegant in appearance,' despite difficult financial circumstances. Friends of the time André Breton, described him as having 'a quality that goes beyond elegance, a truly supreme ease' and Beatrice Wood spoke of his 'truly extraordinary

---

[114] Dubois, 285. This dictionary also lists 'US dressed to the teeth.' To the nines, J.O. Kettridge, *French for English Idioms*, (London Henley, Routeledge and Kegan Paul, 1940, 1976 Edition), 162, Hamilton, Legros, *Dictionnaire International Français Anglais* (Paris Fouraut et Fils, 1880)378, dictionary 'look as if one came out of a bandbox.'

face... everyone who met him loved him.'[115]

Duchamp's explanation of *Pulled at Four Pins*, was "In 1915 I chose a weather vane (rather large) in galvanised iron on which I inscribed *Tiré à quatre épingles M.D. 1915*. I gave this Readymade to Louise Varèse then, and naturally, it has been lost in the course of time.'[116]

Although it was lost, several accounts of it remain, which may give us some clues as to why Duchamp chose it. It was his first American readymade. Breton mentioned it as being amongst other objects in Duchamp's studio 'such as coat hangers, combs, weathercocks, all accompanied by some discordant inscription that served as a title or caption.'[117]

If we decipher this object with Duchamp's method simply asking what is it? And naming it, our response would be '*C'est une girouette'*, It's a weathercock. However, this

---

[115] Schwarz, *The Complete works of Marcel Duchamp*, Volume 1, (London, Thames and Hudson, 1997) 189, from Beatrice Wood, *I Shock Myself*, (Ojai, CA, Dillingham Press, 1985), Breton, 'Marcel Duchamp' in Motherwell Ed., *The Dada Painters and poets: An Anthology*, 1951, trans Ralph Manheim (Boston G.K Hall, 1981), 209.

[116] Arturo Schwarz, Vol. 2., 635. Letter to Schwarz dated September 15 1964.

[117] Schwarz, 635, from "Lighthouse Of the Bride," *View*, New York, Marcel Duchamp Number. vol 5. No.1, March 1945, 8.

phrase is an oft used expression. *'C'est une girouette'* is used to describe an individual who frequently changes opinion.[118] This is like the meaning of a 'weathercock' in English, 'a fickle inconstant, vacillating person.'[119]

Schwarz reads the *girouette* as autobiographical and indicative of Duchamp's ability to adapt to changing circumstances, citing his self-imposed exile due to the war as an example. Duchamp was interested in the writer Laforgue whose version of Hamlet was a parody of Shakespeare's character, a clownish absurd figure who personifies frustration, disillusionment and chronic disenchantment with action in the world.

Gabrielle Buffet-Picabia describes the object as 'some sort of mediaeval casque which was merely a weather vane'[120]. A *casque* in French is a helmet, so the *girouette* would have given the impression of a head turning this way and that[121].

---

[118] Maurice Davau, Marcel Cohen, Maurice Lallemand, *Dictionnaire du francais vivant*, (London Harrap, Boirdas, 1972), 574. Also Hamilton and Legros, *Dictionnaire international Français, Anglais*, (Paris, 1880), 480

[119] J.S.Farmer and W.E.Henley, *Slang and its analogues*, (New York: Arno press, 1970), 308, reprint of 1880-1904 edition of same title.

[120] Schwarz, 635.

[121] Oxford Hachette, entry for *casque*.

Edgar Varèse recounts how the object was lost saying it disappeared when their apartment was sublet. 'This weather vane was in gray (unpainted) tin and it was not a weather vane but one of those round ventilators which are put on chimneys to make them draw better.'[122]

Given Duchamp's love of linguistic nuance, one imagines him learning the English language, and chuckling at the idea of a helmet like object, turning this way and that, a *girouette*, whose function was to make chimney draw better, draw better? What an absurd idea altogether. Who can decide what better drawing is? Once again Duchamp shows us his contempt for judgements.

Draw what? Draw air! The English word for air is a homophone of the French letter *R*. The English pronunciation of the letter R is a homophone of the French word *art*, as in French the last letter is often mute. As Duchamp said 'By simply reading the letters in French, even in any language, some astonishing things happen. Reading the letters, is very amusing.'[123]

Draw better air/art? The *girouette* vacillates this way and

---

[122] Schwarz, 635, letter from Varèse to Schwarz, dated September 15, 1964, Schwarz's translation.
[123] Cabanne, 1979, 63. Duchamp's original words Cabanne 1967, 115, *'on arrive à des choses étonnantes'*, one finds surprising things.

that as it draws better art!

Here a thread appears which traverses Duchamp's oeuvre. The correlation between the pronunciation of the French letter *R*/air interchanged with the English letter R/*art* amplifies Duchamp's punning and wordplay. We will again see the appearance of the R /air in many other works, *Paris Air. Erratum, The Large Glass*, to name just a few.

Duchamp declared 'I like living, breathing better than working...my art would be that of living: each second, each breath is a work which is inscribed nowhere, which is neither visual nor cerebral, it is a sort of constant euphoria.' [124]'I spend my time breathing. I am a *réspirateur* – a breather. I enjoy it tremendously.'[125]

The idea of the art of living is not particular to Duchamp. The French word *art* describes a skill or ability in many domains, particularly before the modern period[126]. The French speak regularly of *les arts de vie,* life arts. These

---

[124] Cabanne, 72.

[125] Thomas Girst, *The Duchamp Dictionary*, (London: Thames and Hudson, 2014) 194, From Anonymous, "Art was a Dream" Interview with Marcel Duchamp, *Newsweek*, vol. 54, no.19, New York, 9 Nov. 1959, 119.

[126] For a history of the word ART see Alain Rey, *Dictionnaire historique de la langue française*, (Paris, Dictionnaires Le Robert, 1992, 119, 120.

include *les arts de bien dire*, the art of diction, *de penser..* of thinking, *...de l'eloquence*, or eloquence etc.[127] Variously one speaks of *'l'art de me plaire*, the art of pleasing me... or not so happily *l'art d'ennuyer tout le monde'*, the art of annoying, or boring everyone... *'il y a un art de marcher, un art de respirer : il y a même un art de se taire* (Valery).*'* [128] There is an art of walking, an art of breathing: there is even an art of staying quiet. This example is from Paul Valery, who was slightly older than Duchamp and a student of Mallarmé, one of Duchamp's much cited influences. Titles from this period include *'L'art d'aimer, L'art de vivre'*, The art of loving, The art of living[129]. These examples shows contemporary language linked the ideas of art and breathing and the art of living.

Other examples from a contemporary dictionary of the expression *Tiré a quatre épingles*, are *'Son caractère était très tire à quatre épingles*, his character was very precise', or *'ce discours est tiré à quatre épingles*, that

---

[127] H. Hamilton et E. Legros, *Dictionnaire International Français Anglais* (Paris: Fouraut et Fils, 1880, 79.

[128] Paul Robert, *Dictionnaire Alphabetique et analogique de la langue française*, (Paris,Société du Nouveau Littré, 1967), 95.

[129]Robert, 95, *L'art de Vivre* is the title of a 1923 second edition publication from Docteur Thoreau. (Paris, Fasquelle, 1923). He notes the abundance of failed artists. 96. He advocates limited expression of emotion.

is a fine spun discourse'[130]. A fine-spun discourse indeed. A historical dictionary says the expression has 'taken on a pejorative tone, when in the 18th century *s'appliquait à qqn vetu avec art'* it applied to someone who was dressed with art/ skill'[131]. This suggests the sense of the French phrase *Tiré à quatre épingles* may have been changing or may have changed when Duchamp used it.

Once again, juxtaposing a title, an *idiotisme*, on a readymade 'work' Duchamp has used an ordinary object to suggest the lack of stability and the absurdity of definition, meaning, and judgement, and the impossibility of translation. The *girouette* suggests a head turning this way and that changing its mind as it draws better air/art.

---

[130] Hamilton, Legros, 378
[131] Rey, *Dictionnaire historique de la langue française*, (Paris, Dictionnaires Le Robert, 1993), 710

À *Bruit Secret*: With Hidden Noise, 1916

Duchamp deliberately fabricated this strange readymade object with Walter Arensberg, one of his patrons who was a very wealthy man. It was a what Duchamp called a *readymade aidé*, a helped readymade. Duchamp was helped in more than one way by Arensberg, and this particular readymade begs to be read. Duchamp had stayed with Arensberg when he first went to New York. Arensberg had inherited his fortune, been to Harvard, and was a poet. Duchamp met many artists, both European and American at Arensberg's home.

Arensberg had what Duchamp described as 'un dada fantastique'... 'a fantastic hobby; cryptography, which consisted of finding the secrets of Dante in the *Divine Comedy* and the secrets of Shakespeare in his plays... He spent his whole life on it...He founded a society...to prove that it was really Bacon who had written Shakespeare's plays...His system was to find, in the text, every three lines allusions to all sorts of things; it was a game for him, like chess, which he enjoyed immensely'[132].

Arensberg left money when he died so that his secretaries could continue these studies. When asked by Cabanne if Duchamp thought Arensberg's work had any validity he said: 'I don't believe so … he twisted words to make them say what he wanted.'[133]

Duchamp asked Arensberg to collaborate with him in making this readymade. He describes how he asked Arensberg to insert an unknown object inside a ball of string which was then enclosed between two metal plates which were then bolted together.

'It's a ball of string between two plates of brass… Walter Conrad Arensberg placed something in the interior of the ball of string without telling me what it was, and I never tried to find out. It was a kind of secret between us and as it made a noise we called the object *Readymade with hidden noise*. Listen to it. I will never know if it's a diamond or a coin.'[134]

---

[132] Cabanne, 51,52.

[133] Cabanne, 51, 52.

[134] Duchamp in *Duchamp du Signe, ecrits*, Flammarion, 1994, 182. *C'est une pélote de ficelle entre deux plaques de cuivre… Walter Conrad Arensberg a placé quelque chose à l'intérieur de la pélote sans me dire ce que c'était, et je n'ai jamais cherché à le savoir. C'était une espèce de secret entre nous et, comme*

As Duchamp felt that this readymade was 'laden with humor' he chose it to be placed on the cover of Breton's *Anthologie de l'humour noir*, published in 1940, but because of the war it was never included on the cover[135].

There are words inscribed onto each of the metal plates. The missing letters form a kind of puzzle which must be deciphered. Duchamp is here clearly referencing Arensberg's preoccupation with deciphering codes[136].

Duchamp said this was "an exercise in comparative orthography (English French) the periods must be replaced (with one exception: Debarrassé[e]) by one of the two letters of the other two lines, but in the same vertical as the period- French and English are mixed and make no 'sense'. The three arrows indicate the continuity of the line from the lower plate to the other [upper] still without meaning" [137]

The words engraved on the brass plates are as follows.

P.G .ECIDES DÉBARASSE.

---

cela faisait un bruit, nous avons l'appelé l'objet readymade à bruit secret. Ecoutez- le. Je ne saurai jamais si c'est un diamant ou une pièce de monnaie.'
[135] Schwarz, p.196.
[136] See Witham, 138.
[137] Schwarz 645, cited from a letter from Duchamp to the author, ca. 1963.

LE. D.SERT F.URNIS.ENT

AS HOW.V.R COR.ESPONDS

Underside with bolts pointing up

.IR. CAR.É   LONGSEA

F.NE, .HEA., .OR.QUE

TE.U S.ARP BAR.AIN

So this gives

Underside:

FIRE CARRE LONGSEA   FIRE SQUARE LONGSEA

FINE CHEAP LORSQUE   FINE CHEAP WHEN

TENU SHARP BARGAIN   HELD SHARP BARGAIN

Top plate:

PEG DECIDES DEBARRASSE PEG DECIDES TO GET RID OF

LES DESERTS FOURNISSENT THE DESERTS PROVIDE

AS HOWEVER CORRESPONDS AS HOWEVER CORRESPONDS

In Duchamp's usual style the objects he has used are, in

slang, endowed with other meanings

A ball of string is called a *pelote*. It may also refer to a fortune, or a ball of yarn.[138] Given Arensberg literally had a fortune and was spending it on deciphering hidden codes, this is clearly what Duchamp was playing at. The *pelote* is held together by two metal plates, which Duchamp himself described as *plaques*. The verb *plaquer* means to pin something against something else. Hence *la pelote est plaquée*. The fortune is pinned. However the verb *plaquer* also means to ditch, dump or abandon[139]. One often speaks of dumping a boyfriend or girlfriend with this verb. *Il l'a plaquée* – he dumped her. Strutz's dictionary example is to '*il a plaqué son job*' he quit his job. The Hachette entry for a US equivalent is '*tout plaquer*, to chuck it all in'. So here Duchamp is clearly insinuating that Arensberg is chucking in his fortune. *La pelote est plaquée*. The fortune is chucked in.

However this is not the end of Duchamp's punning. If we look further we can decipher more. The plates that pin the string so it is enclosed are held together with bolts. In French a bolt is called a *boulon*. The verb *boulonner* means literally to bolt, but also means to slave away at

---

[138] Strutz, 257.
[139] Oxford –Hachette, entry for *plaquer*, Also Strutz, 270.

something. '*Je boulonne toute la journée*. I slave away all day'[140]. So further *la pelote est boulonnée et plaquée*.

Duchamp in his own description of the process of creation of this object asked Arensberg not only to hide the object but in doing so made him bolt the plates together, hence literally in these actions Arensberg was to *boulonner et plaquer la pelote*, bolt and pin the ball of string, or in slang: slave away and chuck in the fortune.

Clearly Duchamp appreciated Arensberg's patronage, but not his hobby of deciphering hidden codes. Here he was slyly 'taking the piss'.

Given Duchamp's penchant for sexual slang it would it be remiss of me not to mention that the verb *peloter* means to feel up in a sexual sense[141]. Perhaps Duchamp was also making a rude suggestion about Arensberg's pastimes suggesting *il se pelote*, he was feeling himself up.

The French words that are completed when the code is deciphered are

CARRE QUAND TENU – literally 'SQUARE WHEN HELD', which is a description of the square plates and form of

---

[140] Strutz, op.cit., p.54 entry for *Boulonner*.
[141] Strutz, Dictionary of French Slang and Colloquial expressions, p.257.

this fabricated readymade *aide*, literally a helped readymade.

But carré also means 'square, frank, outspoken, downright, forthright, straightforward...(personne) plain, blunt, straight(response).'[142]

This gives 'frank when held or kept'. One can be *tenu* in many ways, t*enu responsable*, held to account, one can be '*tenu par*', 'bound by' someone, or '*tenu de faire*' 'obligated to do' something[143]. Duchamp was in many ways bound to Arensberg for his support and patronage, and obligated to put up with his idiosyncrasies.

One can also be '*tenu au secret*', 'held to secrecy'[144]. The French name for this readymade *A bruit secret* is a paronym on the words *bruit* noise and *abri*, shelter. It plays between 'Hidden Shelter' and 'Hidden Noise'. Duchamp gives a nod to their secret, about the object which was hidden inside, whose identity only Arensberg knew, and he gives a nod to the idea of shelter that he had with Arensberg.

---

[142] Dubois, 108.
[143]   https://dictionary.reverso.net/french-english/tenu, accessed 25/09/2019
[144]   https://dictionary.reverso.net/french-english/tenu, accessed 25/09/2019

In returning to the idea of carré meaning frank. If we read this in conjunction with the remainder of the text. '*Les deserts fournissent*' the deserts provide' this gives 'frank when held or kept, the deserts provide'.

It seems to be an ironic statement about being frank about finding treasures in the deserts, a description of Arensberg's searching activities.

Quand is also, in this case, when followed by a word which begins with t, as in *tenu*, a paronym of the word *compte*, so gives *compte tenu*, literally 'taking into account or considering'[145]

Frank considering ... the deserts provide.

No doubt Duchamp knew Arensberg would decipher the missing text, and probably enjoy having their little secret, while Duchamp chuckled to himself.

---

[145]   https://dictionary.reverso.net/french-english/tenu, accessed 25/09/2019

Peigne: Comb, 1916

Peigne is a steel dog's comb, which has an inscription on the back as follows. *2 OU 3 GOUTTES DE HAUTEUR N'ONT RIEN A FAIRE AVEC LA SAUVAGEIRE.*

Firstly, if we follow Duchamp's method and read this readymade through his native language, we can see that the title is not only the name of a comb but is also the subjunctive form of the irregular verb *peindre* to paint. This gives the meaning, succinctly, in the title 'Should I paint?' Thierry de Duve has discussed this philosophically in relation to Duchamp's phrase 'pictorial nominalism'[146].

Peigne, this *read y made* is once again a questioning of definitions. A twentieth century French-English dictionary notes 'artist: *artiste-peintre,* painter N.B. the [French] word *artistes* seems to have a wider meaning than "artists" The English word is seldom used to include musicians or actors.'[147] This designation has recently changed and Anglophones now use the word 'artist' to

---

[146] Thierry De Duve, *Pictorial Nominalism: On Marcel Duchamp's passage from Painting to the readymade*, Minneapolis, Oxford, University of Minnesota Press, 1991.

[147] Marguerite-Marie Dubois, *Dictionnaire modern francais-anglais*, (Paris Larousse, 1960), 46.

cover the arts in general.

Artist, why paint?

Duchamp's readymades are logical reactions to definitions and derive from his suspicion of language. They demonstrate his amusement at the slippage of meaning and the arbitrariness of language.

'I refuse to think about the philosophical clichés that have been renewed every generation since Adam and Eve, and in every corner of the planet. I refuse to think about them, or talk about them, because I don't believe in language. In reality, language, rather than expressing subconscious phenomena, creates thought, with and after word (I openly declare myself to be a "nominalist", at least in this simplified form). All this twaddle – the existence of God, atheism, determinism, free will, societies, death, etc., they're all pieces in a chess game called language, and they're amusing only if you're not concerned about winning or losing this chess game.'[148]

Duchamp provokes thought through his use of words that are hidden in plain sight, teasingly ambiguous or open to

---

[148] Duchamp in Francis M Naumann, Hector Obalk, *Affectt Marcel: The Selected Correspondence of Marcel Duchamp*, translated Jill Taylor, (London, Thames and Hudson, 2000), 348.

play.

Duchamp spoke frequently about definitions of art. His love of dictionaries is evident, as is his skepticism.

"I don't believe in the creative function of the artist. He's a man, like any other. It's his job to do certain things, but the businessman does certain things... On the other hand, the word "art" interests me very much. If it comes from Sanskrit, as I've heard, it signifies "making" ...everyone makes something... those who make things on a canvas with a frame, they're called artists. Formerly they were called craftsmen... [*artisans* in French], a term I prefer... The word artist was invented when the painter became an individual first in monarchical society and then in contemporary society.'[149]

His disdain for painting and even for work led him to rail against the requirement to paint and even more the requirement to make a 'work' of art. When asked by Cabanne 'looking back over your whole life, what satisfies you most?' He replied

'First basically having been lucky. Because basically I've never worked for a living. I consider working for a living slightly imbecilic... I hope that some day we'll be able to

---

[149] Cabanne, 2009, 16

live without being obliged to work. Thanks to my luck I was able to manage without getting wet. [*j'ai pu passer à travers les gouttes*- I was able to pass through the drops, or dodge a bullet.]'[150]

It is clear Marcel didn't see the point in painting, in creating un *oeuvre d'art* a 'work' of art. So the readymade is the next logical step. *Peigne?* Should I paint? No, I will play, with the words, and with people's minds.

Marcel's immersion in a family with an artistic heritage meant he thought about things in terms of art, even though he didn't believe in it:

"It is we who have given the name art to religious things; the word itself doesn't exist among primitives. We have created it for our sole and unique use, it's a little like masturbation. I don't believe in the essential aspect of art.'[151]

'Art's an addictogenic drug – an aesthetic orgasm for the use of a well-fed navel gazing society. You can't even talk about anti-art. You have to declare the failure of the

---

150

https://www.wordreference.com/fren/passer%20à%20travers%20les%20gouttes, accessed 27/09/2019.

[151] Cabanne, 2009, 100.

word "art" and the concept "art", and replace them with a negative, "anart", for the purpose of conversation. On the other hand the artist individual (for the want of another term) exits, has existed, and will always exist, but in very limited numbers, grouped into schools and periods in the history of art which is itself a form of futility.'[152]

Furthermore, his skepticism in relation to the definition of art led him to show the slipperiness of language through his *readymades*.

'He questioned whether art could ever be "adequately defined because the translation of an esthetic emotion into a verbal description is as inaccurate as your description of fear when you have been actually scared.'[153]

The inscription he wrote on the back of the comb demonstrates this slipperiness. It is: 3 ou 4 GOUTTES DE HAUTEUR N'ONT RIEN A FAIRE AVEC LA SAUVAGERIE, literally '3 or 4 drops of height have nothing to do with

---

[152] *Paroles D'artiste, Marcel Duchamp*, (Paris: Editions Fage, 2018), 54.
[153] Thomas Girst, *The Duchamp Dictionary*, London, Thames and Hudson, 2014, 21, cited from "The Western Roundtable on Modern art, San Francisco, 1949, in Clearwater, (ed) 1991, 106.

savagery.'[154] This seems to be a bizarre, nonsensical phrase, but as Duchamp knew, humans try to make 'sense' of everything.

The phonic echoes in this phrase are teasingly evident. Given his disdain for *goût* or taste it would be difficult to ignore the most obvious pun here. This phrase evokes the expression *goût d'auteur*, author's taste. Here he is becoming not a painter but an author. This gives: '3 or 4 author's tastes have nothing to do with savagery'. Furthermore the word *hauteur* may also mean nobility or haughtiness, and *sauvagerie* may mean unsociability.[155] Hence we may read '3 or 4 drops of nobility have nothing to so with savagery', or '3 or 4 drops of haughtiness have nothing to do with savagery', or alternatively 'unsociability'.

Duchamp was delighted with this readymade:

'During the 48 years since it was chosen as a readymade this little iron comb had kept the characteristics of a true Readymade: no beauty, no ugliness, nothing particularly

---

[154] Calvin Tomkins hears an echo of *Stephane Mallarmés* poem *Un coup de dés jamais n'abolira le hazard*. A throw of the dice will never abolish chance. Tomkins, *Marcel Duchamp a biography*, (New York Henry Holt, 1996), 160.

[155] Oxford Hachette, entries for *hauteur* and *sauvagerie*,

aesthetic about it ... it was not even stolen in all these 48 years'[156].

This recalls his statement about the choice of the readymades:

The choice of the readymades was never dictated by esthetic delectation. This choice was based on a reaction of visual indifference with at the same time a total absence of good or bad taste [...] in fact a complete anesthesia.'[157]

Despite this visual indifference and Duchamp's desired lack of feeling, there is always a sentiment of humour.

Peigne recalls one of Duchamp's early cartoons, in which a man is standing doing his hair whilst looking into a mirror. A seated woman says to the standing one : *Ce que t'es long a te peigner* – It takes you so long to comb your hair. The standing man responds *La critique est aisée mais la raie difficile*. Criticism is easy, but the parting is difficult. *La raie* is a homophone of *l'art est*.. Hence this is also a pun on the expression *La critique est aisée mais*

---

[156] Schwarz, Vol 2 643. From d'Harnoncourt McShine Eds, Marcel Duchamp. 279.,
[157] *Paroles D'artiste, Marcel Duchamp,* (Paris Editions Fage,2018) 30.

l'art est difficile, Criticism is easy but art is difficult[158].

With *Peigne / Comb*, Duchamp is carrying on the theme from one of this first humourous drawings. We should never forget Duchamp was first and foremost a humourous artist.[159]

---

[158] Duchamp is paraphrasing the eighteenth-century playwright Philippe Néricault Destouche, from *Le Glorieux*.
[159] Cartoon dated 1909, Schwarz, 521

Pliant de voyage: Traveler's folding item, 1916

This is the cover of a typewriter emblazoned with the name of a manufacturer Underwood.

One must be aware that the typewriter was a relatively new invention at the time. Typing pools were a new site of employment for women and a large percentage of employed women worked in them. Salacious behavior by male colleagues was rife. The Underwood typewriter was one of the first with which the typist could see what she was typing as she typed[160]. So she could see what she was doing.

Travelers folding item was first exhibited in *The exhibition of Modern art*, in Bourgeois galleries New York April 3-29, 1916. It was not labelled in the catalogue, there was simply mention of "Two Readymades" by Marcel Duchamp. He was evasive about where it was exhibited saying simply "My readymades were exhibited

---

[160] Wikipaedia, entry for typewriter. https://en.wikipedia.org/wiki/Typewriter accessed 10/08/2019

in the umbrella stand."[161] Schwarz speculates that 'perhaps it was hooked over the protruding knob of some elaborate hallstand in the foyer. Duchamp was probably happy that no-one had noticed his readymades, as this meant they had no esthetic emanation.[162]

When asked why he had chosen this item as a readymade Duchamp said " I thought it would be a good idea to introduce softness into the readymades- in other words not altogether hardness, porcelain or iron or things like that ... so that's why the typewriter cover came into existence.'[163]

Naumann has claimed the title allowed Duchamp to make a pun on a Paris salon exhibition category of *sous-bois*, literally underwood.[164]

The original has been lost but Duchamp had copies made for the *Boîte en valise*, his portable museum, and created copies for Schwarz. The miniature replica was displayed

---

[161] Schwarz, 646, citation from Marcel Jean, *Marcel Duchamp Briefe an, Lettres à Letters to Marcel Jean*, Munich silke Schreiber, 1987, p.77.

[162] Tomkins, *Duchamp A biography*, (New York, Henry Holt, 1996), 162.

[163] Duchamp in 1953, Schwarz, 646. Cited rom D'Harnoncourt McShine, 281

[164] Here he cites Caumont and Gough-Cooper, however it is doubtful such category of 'undergrowth' painting existed, and as the date for this entry is 1 April, 1916 I suspect this is a joke on the part of Gough-Cooper and Caumont.

on the left-hand side of the *Boite* above the urinal in such a way to emphasize its skirt like quality.

The inscription of the name UNDERWOOD and the skirt like appearance begs an easy English suggestive pun, underwould -one would look under if possible. If one were to go further one could note in Duchamp's usual vulgar way that a wood or a woody is an American euphemism for an erection, hence extending the idea of a desire for sexual activity. [165] The French title pliant de voyage also suggests the English word pliant, meaning a malleable person. The French *plier* can also mean to submit.[166] One imagines this suggestion of a malleable or submissive person on a voyage and the suggestion of a skirt through this typewriter cover must have pleased Duchamp.

---

[165] Richard A Spears, McGraw Hill, *Dictionary of American Slang and Colloquial expressions*, New York, 2007 p.402. woody 'an erection of the penis. His morning woody made a little mountain with the sheets on his bed.'

[166] Hachette Oxford Dictionary for Windows, entry for *plier*, to give in or yield.

Apolinère Enameled, 1916-17

This *readymade aidé* or 'helped readymade' is a picture on metal of a young girl painting a bed in a small room with a dresser and mirror and slightly open curtains. The bed has a strange perspective about it which resembles an impossible drawing as Duchamp has blocked out part of one of the horizontal bars so that it does not connect with the end of the bed. It gives the illusion of being a three- dimensional object but the missing section means it would not function if it were real.

Duchamp said of this 'work':

I changed the lettering in an advertisement for 'sapolin paints' misspelling intentionally the name of Guillaume Apollinaire and also adding the reflection of the little girl's hair in the mirror. I am sorry Apollinaire never saw it, he died in 1918 in France.'[167]

He also added a strange cryptic text where the manufacturer's name was previously. The manufacturer's

---

[167] Schwarz, 648, from D'Harnoncourt Mc Shine, 280.

name was previously GERSTENDORFER BROS. NEW YORK USA. Duchamp has changed this to ANY ACT RED BY HER TEN OR EPERGNE NEW YORK USA[168].

The spelling of Apollinaire's name in this work is APOLINÈRE. An *ère* is an era, and also the homophone of *aire*, and the letter *R* in French, the letter Duchamp plays with constantly in his oeuvre, in both English and French for its homophonic qualities.[169]The English letter R is a homophone of the French word *art*. In drawing attention to this change Duchamp is emphasizing the change from *aire*, to *ère*.

Apollinaire had accompanied Duchamp on his 1912 trip to the Jura with Francis Picabia and Gabrielle Buffet Picabia, Francis Picabia's current wife. Apollinaire then had just written his poem *Zone*, which was published in 1913, and was to become his most celebrated work, his last poem. Zone celebrates Paris and modernity with a nostalgic view of religion. The Jura was a frontier zone. A *Zone* may be a frontier, a slum, and erogenous zone and a neighbourhood and his title and the poem plays on all

---

[168] Schwarz, Vol 2, 647,648
[169] Oxford Hachette entry for ère.

these meanings[170]. Apollinaire's poem Zone is written in free verse, in which the sound and lack of punctuation open interpretation.

An *aire* is a zone, or an area[171]. In emphasizing this change in Apollinaire's name Duchamp is playing with the homophones *ère*, era, *aire*, zone, *air*, a tune or song, and the French letter *R*. When Duchamp plays with the letter *R*, we cannot ignore his association of this letter with the English R, a homophone of the French word *art*. Duchamp suggest Apollin*aire*'s *Zone* is art. The art of an era. *L*'R *d'une ère*. It is a touching tribute to Apollinaire.

Schwarz has noted that Duchamp considered himself to be a poet rather than a painter and identified with Apollinaire as he was such, and Schwarz has indicated similarities between their works[172].

Apollinaire coined several new terms in relation to the arts, the most significant was surrealism, *surrealisme*, which he used in a letter to Paul Dermée in March 1917, and then in the preface for the Ballet *Parade*, which

---

[170]   David   Lehman   translator https://www.vqronline.org/translations/apollinaires-zone, accessed 4/10/19. Littré 1900, 1294.
[171] Oxford Hachette entry for *aire*
[172] Schwarz, 197. Vol 1

opened in May 1917.[173]   The performance of Parade caused a scandal, much of it because of Picasso's sets.

The scandal continued with Erik Satie being sued by a journalist who had given a bad review. Satie had sent him a postcard with the following, *"Monsieur et cher ami – vous êtes un cul, un cul sans musique! Signé Erik Satie"* ("Sir and dear friend – you are an arse, an arse without music! Signed, Erik Satie.") Jean Cocteau also yelled *cul*, arse, throughout the court hearing[174].

Apollinaire was not one to avoid vulgar language, He wrote several pornographic novels, His novel *Les Onze Mille Verges, The Ten Thousand Rods*, or *Penises*, is a pun on the Catholic veneration of the *Onze Mille Vierges, The Ten Thousand Virgins*. Apollinaire transforms the word vierges, virgins into *verges* penises, with the slip of an 'l'

---

[173]https://en.wikipedia.org/wiki/Guillaume_Apollinaire, accessed 4/10./19 "All things considered, I think in fact it is better to adopt surrealism than supernaturalism, which I first used" [*Tout bien examiné, je crois en effet qu'il vaut mieux adopter surréalisme que surnaturalisme que j'avais d'abord employé*] Cited from Jean-Paul Clébert, *Dictionnaire du surréalisme*, A.T.P. & Le Seuil, Chamalières, p. 17, 1996. The surrealist movement did not really emerge until 3 years later.
[174] https://en.wikipedia.org/wiki/Parade_%28ballet%29, cited from Austin, William W. Music in the 20th Century. New York. W. W. Norton, 1966. Library of Congress Catalog Card No. 64-18776 and Mary E Davis Erik Satie, New York Reaktion Books, 2007, 120.

and in his novel celebrates diverse forms of sexuality[175].

Given Apollinaire's pornographic output, the bed is obviously an erotic site, and the young girl a very young virgin. The phallic nature of the post she is gently painting has also been noted. Another pun is evident. When Apollinaire is pronounced in English with a French accent, it sounds like 'a pole in air.'[176] This is all the more emphasized by the way Duchamp painted out of one section of the bed to make one of the poles of the bed stand upright, unattached to the horizontal of the bed frame to make it an impossible object.

There are similarities between Apollinaire's play of 24 June 1917 *Les Mamelles de Tiresias*, The *Nipples of Tiresias*, and Duchamp's works. *Les Mamelles de Tiresias* was written in 1903 but modified for its 1917 performance. Apollinaire subtitled the play *Drame Surrealiste*. It is inspired by the classic story of Tiresias the soothsayer of Greek mythology. Apollinaire's character Theresa changes gender to become Tiresias in order to promote equality of the sexes and promote antimilitarism. Her breasts become balloons that float

---

[175]   Reverso,   https://dictionary.reverso.net/french-english/verge, accessed 4/10/19
[176]
https://www.toutfait.com/unmaking_the_museum/Apolinere%20enameled.html, accessed 15/10/2019

away and she grows a moustache and a beard. She forces her husband to adopt female dress and produce children. He produces 40 050 babies in one day. In the second act she throws a urinal out a window. The play caused an uproar, due to its references to France's lack of children and the war and was widely reported in the press. Apollinaire had adopted a female persona in 1909, Louise Lalanne.[177]

Duchamp's provocation with a urinal in *Fountain*, later in 1917 and his adoption of a female character *Rrose Selavy* in 1920 certainly have similarities with Apollinaire's play. His use of a moustache on his 1919 punning Mona Lisa with inscription *LHOOQ* [letters pronounced as *elle a chaud au cul*, she has a hot arse], may also be a reference to Apollinaire who had been implicated in the theft of the Mona Lisa and was arrested as a suspect. He was released a week later. Apollinaire's former secretary, Honoré Pieret stole statues from the Louvre, but the Mona Lisa was stolen by an Italian housepainter Vincent Peruggia, caught 2 years later. Apollinaire implicated his friend Picasso, who was also brought in for questioning in the

---

[177] Schwarz, 197. Schwarz reads this work in relation to Alchemical symbols.

theft of the Mona Lisa, but exonerated. [178]

The text ANY ACT RED BY HER TEN OR EPERGNE is a puzzle. An epergne is an anglicized name for a table centre piece which is often used to hold fruit or flowers[179]. Whatever Duchamps' phrase may mean, if it means anything at all, it is worth noting that an epergne in French is called a *surtout*, echoing Apollinaire's newly coined term *surrealist*.[180] *Surtout* means literally 'above all', or 'especially'. Furthermore, a surtout is in English a type of *manteau* or overcoat, from the words *sur*, over, *tout*, everything[181]. We will see this *manteau*, coat theme reappear in Duchamp's *Trebuchet, Trap* later in 1917.

Epergne echoes the words '*et peigne*', 'and comb', of the *Peigne*, comb, 'work' from earlier in 1916. *Epergne* may also mean spare, as in to have a spare, meaning reserve or extra. [182]

---

[178]https://en.wikipedia.org/wiki/Guillaume_Apollinaire, accessed 4/10/19 from Richard Lacayo, *"Art's Great Whodunit: The Mona Lisa Theft of 1911"*, *Time*, 27 April 2009.
[179] *Oxford Reference Dictionary*, Eds Judy Pearsall, Bill Trumble, (London, New York, Oxford, 1995), 472.
[180] https://en.wikipedia.org/wiki/Epergne, accessed 4/10/19, also *Le Nouveau Littre*, (Paris, Editions Garnier, 2005), 1675
[181] *Oxford English reference Dictionary*, Eds Judy Pearsall and Bill Trumble, (Oxford, Oxford University Press, 1995) 1423
[182] https://en.wikipedia.org/wiki/Epergne, accessed 4/10/19

Perhaps this *epergne*, or spare which recalls the *manteaux* and the *peigne* is, in fact a spare, in case we miss the hints Duchamp gives us elsewhere.

Epergne, is derived from the French word *epargne*, meaning saving.[183] The *epargne* in slang refers to the *cagnotte*, or the kitty that players use when gambling.[184]

It is difficult to over-look the homophone of red, read, in this phrase.

Whatever the meaning of this phrase may be, whatever we may have read, Duchamp certainly has us where he wants us, searching for meaning, teasing out ambiguities and trying to make sense of his 'work'.

Apollinaire's poetry was extremely inventive and experimental. His Calligrammes, begun in 1913, form shapes, such as a heart, or a mirror, with the letters of the text itself, a complete innovation for the time. He used overheard phrases in his poetry rather like vocal

---

[183] *Oxford English reference Dictionary*, Eds Judy Pearsall and Bill Trumble, (Oxford, Oxford University Press, 1995) 472.

[184] Jules Lermina, Henri Leveque, *Dictionnaire Francais Argot, à l'usage des gens du monde qui veulent parler correctement la langue verte*, [*French Slang dictionary for worldly people who want to speak slang correctly*]. (Paris, Les Editions de Paris, 1991 reproduction de l'edition du meme nom de 1900 Chez Chacornac), 60.

readymade phrases[185]. His *Caligrammes, poems of love and war 1913-16*, were published posthumously.

Apollinaire's stated: 'It will perhaps be reserved for an artist as disengaged from aesthetic preoccupations, as occupied with energy as Marcel Duchamp, to reconcile Art and the people.' Duchamp's reaction to this when asked by Cabanne was 'What a joke! That's all Apollinaire, I wasn't very important in the group, so he said to himself, "I have to write a little about him, about his friendship with Picabia"... Apollinaire had guts, he saw things and imagined others which were very good, but that is his assertion not mine.'[186]

We should not forget Duchamp loved *langue verte*, slang, colorful language, humor and those who used them.

---

[185] Schwarz, 197.
[186] Cabanne, 2009, 37

Selected Bibliography

Antliff, Mark, Particia Dee Leighton, *Cubism and Culture*, (London, Thames and Hudson, 2001)

Apollinaire, Guillaume, *Marcel Duchamp*, (Paris L'Echoppe, 1994) Preface Jean Suquet.

Ashton, Doré, *Rencontre avec Marcel Duchamp*, (Paris, L'Echoppe) 1996.

Bourdieu, Pierre, *The Field of Cultural Production: Essays on Art and Literature*, Ed and Intro by Randal Johnson, (Cambridge, Polity Press, 1993).

Brooke, Peter, http://www.peterbrooke.org.uk/a&r/Du%20Cubisme/Part%20two/duchamp, accessed 19/09/2019

Cabanne, Pierre, *Dialogues with Marcel Duchamp, with an appreciation by Jasper Johns*, (New York Da Capo Press, 2009) reprint of Belfond Press 1979 Edition of same name,) translation Ron Padgett.

Cabanne, Pierre, Entretiens, avec Marcel Duchamp, (Paris, Editions Belfond, 1967)

Colin, Philippe, *Marcel Duchamp Parle des Readymades*,

(Paris: L'Échoppe, 2008)

De Duve, Thierry, *Pictorial Nominalism : On Marcel Duchamp's Passage from Painting to the Readymade*, (Minneapolis, Oxford, University of Minnesota Press, 1991. Foreword John Rajchman, translation Dana Polan and author.

Dubois, Marguerite-Marie, *Dictionnaire modern Français-Anglais*, (Paris, Larousse, 1960)

Duchamp, Marcel, *Notes*, (Paris: Flammarion, 1999) compiled Paul Matisse, preface Pontus Hulten.

Duchamp, Marcel, *Duchamp du signe, Ecrits, Réunis et présentés par Michel Sanouillet*, (Paris, Champs Flammarion, 1975, 1994) Revue et augmentée avec la collaboration de Elmer Peterson

Duchamp, Marcel, *Duchamp du Signe suivi de Notes*, revue et corrigé Anne Sanouillet, Anne, Paul B Franklin (Paris: Flammarion, 2008)

Duchamp, Marcel, *The Writings of Marcel Duchamp*, (New York, Da Capo Press, 1973) Michel Sanouillet, Michel, translations Elmer Peterson.

Gervais, Andre, *La Raie Alitée d'effets: à propos of Marcel Duchamp*, (Hurtubise, Quebec, la Salle, HMH,

1984)

Albert Gleizes, Albert, Metzinger, Jean, *Du Cubisme*, (Paris: Eugène Figuières, 1912, reedition, Presence, 1980)

Girst, Thomas, *The Duchamp Dictionary*, (London: Thames and Hudson, 2014)

Goldfarb Marquis, Alice, *Marcel Duchamp: The Bachelor Stripped Bare*, (Boston, Massachusetts, MFA Publications, 2002)

Gough Cooper, Jennifer; Caumont, Jacques; *Marcel Duchamp work and life: Ephemerides on and about Marcel Duchamp and Rrose Selavy*, (Massachusetts, MIT Press, 1993)

Guiraud, Pierre, *Les Locutions Françaises*, (Paris, Presses Universitaires de France, 1973)

Foucault, Michel, "7Propos sur le 7eme Ange", *La Grammaire Logique, La Science de Dieu*, Paris, Claude Tchou Editeur, 1970

Franklin, Paul B, "Headline Duchamp" *Etant Donné*, no.7. 2006, 140-171.

J'aime Rire, (Paris, Bayard, no.14) 2019,

Kettridge, J.O. *French for English Idioms and Figurative Phrases*, (London, Routledge and Kegan Paul, 1940, 1996 reprint)

Kuh, Katherine, *The Artist's voice, Talks with Seventeen Modern Artists*, (New York, Da Capo Press, 2000 republication of Harper and Row's 1962 Edition)

Lehman,David, https://www.vqronline.org/translations/apollinaires-zone,

Marcadé, Bernard, *La vie à credit*, (Paris, Flammarion, 2007)

Motherwell Ed., *The Dada Painters and poets: An Anthology*, 1951, trans Ralph Manheim (Boston G.K Hall, 1981).

Naumann, Francis M, Hector Obalk, *Affect Marcel: The Selected Correspondence of Marcel Duchamp*, translated Jill Taylor, (London, Thames and Hudson, 2000)

Rabaté, Jean Michel, "Duchamp's Ego", *Textual Practice*, 2010, 18:2, 229

Roussel, Raymond, *Comment J'ai ecrit certains de mes*

livres, (Paris, Gallimard, 1979)

Sanouillet, Michel, "Marcel Duchamp and the French intellectual tradition", *Marcel Duchamp*, Eds. Anne D'Harnoncourt, Kynaston McShine, (New York: Museum of Modern Art, 1973, 1989)

Semin, Didier, *Duchamp : Le Paradigm du dessin d'humour*, Kunsthalle Marcel Duchamp, 2015

Shearer,   Rhonda   Roland
https://www.toutfait.com/issues/issue_3/collections/rrs/shearer.htm

Thompson, Glyn, Julian Spalding, "Did Marcel Duchamp Steal Elsa's Urinal" *The Art Newspaper, International Edition* issue 262, 3 Nov 2014.

Thoreau, Docteur, *L'art de Vivre* (Paris, Fasquelle, 1923).

Tomkins, Calvin, *Duchamp a biography*, (New York, Henry Holt and Company, 1996)

Tomkins, Calvin, *Marcel Duchamp: the afternoon Interviews*, (New York: Badlands unlimited, 2013)

Toutfait,   unattributed:
https://www.toutfait.com/unmaking_the_museum/Pharmacy.html

https://www.toutfait.com/unmaking_the_museum/Apol
inere%20enameled.html,

Wikipedia

https://en.wikipedia.org/wiki/Typewriter 10/08/2019

https://en.wikipedia.org/wiki/Guillaume_Apollinaire,

https://en.wikipedia.org/wiki/Parade_%28ballet%29,

https://en.wikipedia.org/wiki/Epergne,

Witham, Larry, *Pablo Picasso, Marcel Duchamp and the Battle for the soul of Modern Art*, (Hanover and London, New England Press, 2013)

Dictionaries:

Collins Gem Spanish dictionary, (Glasgow, Harper Collins, 2006)

Davau, Maurice, Marcel Cohen, Marcel, Maurice Lallemand, *Dictionnaire du francais vivant*, (London Harrap, Boirdas, 1972),

Denoeu, François, David Sices, David, Jacqueline Sices, *2001 French and English idioms* 2nd Edition, 2001 *Idiotismes francais et anglais,* , (New York, Barron, Hauppauge, 2nd Edition, 1996)

Farmer, J.S, W.E. Henley, *Slang and its analogues*, (New York: Arno press, 1970), reprint of 1880-1904 edition of same title.

Hamilton, H, Legros, E, *Dictionnaire Internationale français anglais*, (Paris, Ch Fouraut et Fils, Paris, Samson Low et Co. London, 1880)

Larousse, *Dictionnaire du Francais Argotique et Populaire*, (Paris, Larousse, 2006)

Lermina, Jules ; Henri Leveque, *Dictionnaire francais-argot à l'usage des gens du monde qui veulent parler correctement la langue Verte*, (Paris, Les Editions de Paris, 1991, reprint of Edition same name Paris Charcornac, 190

Littré, Emile, *Dictionnaire de la langue francaise*, (Paris Hachette et Cie, 1883),

Littré, E et Beaujean, A, *Dictionnaire de la langue Francaise de E Littré*, (Paris Hachette, 1900)

Le Nouveau Littré, (Paris, Editions Garnier, 2005)

Oxford Hachette French English Dictionary for windows, 1994-1996, entry for *champ*.

Pearsall, Judy, Trumble, Bill, Eds. *Oxford Reference*

Dictionary, (London, New York, Oxford, 1995),

https://dictionary.reverso.net/french-english/verge,

https://dictionary.reverso.net/french-english/tenu,

Rey, Alain *Dictionnaire historique de la langue française*, (Paris, Dictionnaires Le Robert, 1993)

Rey, Alain, Sophie Chantreau, *Dictionnaire d'expressions et locutions*, (Paris : Le Robert, 2003)

Robert, Paul, *Dictionnaire Alphabetique et analogique de la langue française*, (Paris, Société du Nouveau Littré, 1967)

Spears, Richard A, *Dictionary of American Slang and Colloquial expressions*, (New York, McGraw Hill, 2007)

Strutz, Henri, *Dictionary of French Slang and Colloquial expressions*, (New York, Barron, 2009)

https://www.wordreference.com/fren/passer%20à%20tr avers%20les%20gouttes

About the Author

Lyn Merrington is an Australian artist, and art-historian. The germ for this publication began in 1998 when beginning a PhD with an interest in Duchamp's linguistic techniques. In depth study of the literary figures that were important for Duchamp ensued. Many years of linguistic study and French immersion were essential for the completion of this study. Lyn has visited the major Duchamp sties in France, Spain and the United States.

Lyn is a visual artist with an interest in landscape, weather and ephemeral changes, and occasionally portraiture. Major art series include 'Infinity samplers' and 'Rainbow Basking' begun in 1995. Lyn works both in public art and the private domain.